The Sol Plaatje European Union
Poetry Anthology

Volume V

The Sol Plaatje European Union Poetry Anthology

Volume V

Selected by Johann de Lange,
Goodenough Mashego and Joan Metelerkamp

The views and opinions expressed in this publication are not necessarily those of the funder.

First published by Jacana Media (Pty) Ltd in 2015

10 Orange Street
Sunnyside
Auckland Park 2092
South Africa
+2711 628 3200
www.jacana.co.za

© Individual authors, 2014

All rights reserved.

ISBN 978-1-4314-2245-6

Cover design by Shawn Paikin
Set in Ehrhardt 11/13pt
Printed and bound by Bidvest Data
Job no. 002584

Also available as an e-book:
d-PDF ISBN 978-1-4314-2246-3
ePUB ISBN 978-1-4314-2247-0
mobi file ISBN 978-1-4314-2248-7

See a complete list of Jacana titles at www.jacana.co.za

Contents

Foreword *Dr Mongane Wally Serote*.................ix
Message from the ambassador *Roeland van de Geer*...xviii

Baleka, What do You Know of Tenders and Thieves? Or
   Cockroaches for that Matter? *Jim Pascual Agustin*...1
Veins Cut Open *Jim Pascual Agustin*.................4
December in Paris *Karin Andersen*...................5
The Thursday market *Karin Andersen*................7
die pad na Klipfontein *Carel Aäron Anthonissen*.......8
Afrika-les *Caroline F Archer*.......................10
The Phone Call *Saleeha Idrees Bamjee*..............12
Who will? *Fadwah Booley*.........................13
Aleen *Steven Bresler*..............................14
Portrait of a Mother and Indiscretion
   Sindiswa Busuku-Mathese........................15
Veldmeens se lied: *Arthur Benjamin Cloete*..........16
Austin Roberts Voëlpark *Eckhard Cloete*............19
by die dood van Mikhail Kalashnikof *Eckhard Cloete*..20
natuurlewe, afrika *Eckhard Cloete*.................22
Die Kaper-naar *Leonard Etienne Cloete*.............23
A Short Guide to Death *Margaret Clough*...........24
OLD POET *Margaret Clough*.....................25
Heritage Site *Christine M Coates*..................26
Mapungubwe *Christine M Coates*.................28
Bruidjie van Jemen *Corné Coetzee*..................29
Platipuspaddas *Corné Coetzee*.....................30
Performance Scale *Genna Gardini*.................31
Die boekanier van Muckleneuk *Sunelle Geyer*.......39
Jo'burg, My Darling *Shawn Greyling*...............40

City Night *Kerry Hammerton* 42
Die moppie van my DNA *Suenel Holloway* 43
A letter from the dead *Morwamphaka Maisella
   Sello Huma*................................ 45
Dipšišamare tša Marikana *Morwamphaka
   Maisella Sello Huma*........................ 46
For my brother *Musawenkosi Khanyile* 47
Mother *Musawenkosi Khanyile*.................... 49
eenvoud *Lara Kirsten*........................... 50
Okungenani *Thandanani Christopher Mabaso* 51
Sola gape *Katise Mawela* 52
Kuyoze Kube Nini *Mokoena Mlondolozi*............ 53
Lenhlupheko Izondlula
   Mokoena Mlondolozi......................... 55
Ngaphambi Kwezifungo
   Mokoena Mlondolozi......................... 56
Dinaledi Tse Ntlenyana *Thabiso Michael Mofokeng*.... 59
Ke Hopotse Heso *Thabiso Michael Mofokeng* 61
Tsietsi Mashinini *Tsietsi Mokhele* 65
mad as a broken dish *Che Kgahliso Moshesh* 66
eskom na gezi - eskom and power *Moses Mtileni*...... 67
We Have Come *Moses Mtileni* 68
MYEKENI UMNTU UKUBA ANIMAZI *Madoda
   Ndlakuse*.................................... 69
Keeping His Shoes *Pamela Newham*................ 71
Lost Girls *Pamela Newham* 72
And Soon *Mzu Nhlabatsi*........................ 73
Mathapelo *Sizakele Nkosi* 74
The mad man *Sizakele Nkosi*..................... 75
I know this *Zukisani Nongogo*.................... 77
I remember when *Zukisani Nongogo* 81
"Promise from the Elders" *Lazola Pambo*.......... 82
Granny. Called 'Ma' *Francine Simon* 83

Licence *Francine Simon* 84
Tea *Francine Simon* 85
Lament for the Stones *Annette Snyckers* 86
Stopover *Annette Snyckers* 87
The Button Tin *Annette Snyckers* 88
Rorschach Liggaam *David C Steyn* 90
postpartum *Gisela Ullyatt* 91
vir 'n uiltuin *Gisela Ullyatt* 92
Streetclass Diseases *Athol Williams* 94
illegal *Sue Woodward* 95
Straatkindnar,'n skildery *Frank Wright* 96

Biographies 97
What is the European Union (EU)? 110

Foreword

Here in South Africa, poems are still being sung and performed. For some time now, a new generation of poets, men and women, have been doing that; they sing and perform poetry, almost in the same way as it was done long ago. For some reason, which is still very difficult to know or understand, when the colonialists arrived and found the performed and sung poetry, they called it praise poetry, perhaps meaning the same thing as they call African art, arts and craft. Nowadays when people refer to rap, they, I think, are referring to performed and sung poetry. The real name of this genre in Sesotho is *Dithoko*. Soon, rather than later, South Africans must begin to speak at least three languages: an African language of their choice, Afrikaans and English. You cannot live among people and not hear or understand what they are saying. Here is poetry, in this *The Sol Plaatje European Union Poetry Anthology Volume V*, which is South African in both context and content.

In the silence of this immovable time, people pick up silent messages which speak loudly. It is especially so, when it is matters of death or life: when death happens or life happens, as we all know, there are many types of deaths as there are many types of lives. Both are an issue of change, which is permanent in the universe. The poets in this collection, without fail, all cast their eyes far and wide across our country, and even at times across the world and its people. They have learnt a lot about their country and people and even as they are at the tip, at the end of the earth, they have also learnt about the people of the world.

Experiencing the poetry in this collection tells one that it would not be surprising if we were to learn that poetry and crying were created on the same day. Or that, if you do not know what crying is you would not know anything about laughing. That is how hard the collection of poems in this anthology are. The poems are similar, as if to confirm that this is one other trait which describes peers. They are also very different, as if to confirm that no two things are ever similar. I do not know where all of these poets come from in our country, however, I get a sense that they come from far-flung corners of South Africa.

They are black (Africans, coloureds, and Indians) to use a Black Consciousness parlance, and they are also white, if ever there was such a human colour. They are all South Africans, I suspect. Or, they have experienced that texture, that unique being, that fingerprint of being South African, which is busy shaping in us even as we are not aware that it does and perhaps, even as we would prefer it were not so. It is like *Eish!* on our tongues. In their being different and also being similar, it is as they enter who we are as a people; and it is when they find our spirit and explore it. That is the moment when the poets' word become the writing on the wall. The poets in this anthology have written on the wall. Let us read the writing on the wall.

One poet says:
"Abeeda's toothless mouth sprays saliva as/ she paints a picture of her thirteen years/ on Cape town streets. He feels her spit in his face, on his nose, on his lip, arousing/ his middleclass concern over streetclass/ diseases."

What kind of a country breeds people who say things like this? This is spooky maan!

Another poet says:
"My mother smells of indiscretion/ in fact she smells of strange/ things. Not Camphor or Zam Buk/ not of anything familiar.

My mother walks slowly,/ crossing the bedroom in high-/ heeled shoes. In my grey window I see the sky. In the sky the moon/ is round. She hides her smile behind the curtain lace and/ whispers, 'My child sees everything'."

Something has gone drastically wrong when the poets or singers speak about their country's people; they do not spare them. Not only that but also, when the words are so vitriolic, as to even undress them in public without a flinch. Then, this thing which is called compassion has been scraped to the bottom, even what must perplex us with its metaphors is empty, what remains is utter nakedness.

And yet another poet says:
"If food is scarce, adolescence cockroaches can live on a very reliable resource – their parents' faeces." [1]

"There are lessons that a parent/ can teach a child. The first few steps,/ how to listen, read and write. Seldom/ how to be tender as you plunder/ and rape, how to deal with the spoils,/ the leftovers, something sharp/ scraping the bottom."

There is a very controlled anger in almost all of the poems in this book. If we recall, that anger is also a form of helplessness, so how can it be expressed in controlled voices and in carefully chosen words? What do the poets want?; what has not been done?; what is the future to be and how must it be lived, if the writing on the wall is so unsparing and so brutal?; does someone hear, think and understand what is being and what has been said here? No one can be beyond the comment of these razor-sharp, but subtle and quiet, almost unsaid words on the wall!

No one has been insulted here, but that is because everyone has been insulted. That is because if one of us says, "… that is not me …" then everyone will say "… that is not me …" and if we were all then to say "… who is it then …" the silence will look at us; it will stare at us, eyeball to eyeball. What is the matter? Is it true that the voices of poets are evidence of things unsaid, but known and not spoken about?

There is a history of that in this country; we heard things like that before; and because those things became our consciousness, they ended up being our actions. How does evidence or experience become a teacher? Or, in other words, what is the use of poets and their poetry in a nation? The poets do what they know best – poetry; some go further than that as they act out their poems. Is that the reason why poets in our country sing and perform their poems? What do we do when they do that? We cannot sit there quietly because, if we do, it means we are done.

When some sing or perform their poetry, they make lots of noise or overact; many sing and perform but control their bodies, voices and words. They are many too. They make you walk out of where they were performing, thinking.

Hear the poet say here:
"Scientists claim some female cockroaches prefer weaker partners because they like gentle sex.

A University of Manchester team has concluded stronger male cockroaches are too aggressive and often injure their partners."[2]

"There are consequences, you say, / for not heeding the pliant rod / of your word. In a chamber echoing an empty order, no king / will want to speak. So you had to / stamp your

feet without grinding/ your teeth this time around./ A flick of your hand and the beating/ instantly began."

For anyone to defy, courage is needed because defiance is a declaration of war. War is very untidy. Yet, many times, human beings choose it. It is not only untidy it is also very tough. It is so because both sides hurt from it.

Hear this other poet:
"She (Mother) tells of her walk with her god, her simple/ life beneath bridges, clearly boasting/ about her immunity to his diseases./ He offers her cash. She scoffs and carries on digging/ through the garbage bin where he found her."

And then this poet again:
"My mother is an old woman./ she/ is no longer young. Yet I smell/ her indiscretion. I have smelt it/ on her for days. She has been laughing and smiling without/ restraint."

Why is it that, at times, poets do not see beauty in life? It is because they have to learn other things, so that they must know what is relative to those which are ugly. The poets in this collection of poems are searching, again and again, and searching for hope. They are searching for what is hope because they do not know it in flesh; they remember it, they know they know it. We are all here with them.

Somewhere here I said that the poets in this anthology are very far flung in their reach. They reach all the corners of our country and so also reach the corners of the world. Even there faraway, as they search and search and search they cannot find the staff of life. It is said that what you cannot find out there is what you cannot find there inside you. That is what the poets are saying through their writings on the wall. We must in stillness face this wall and the writing on it. That is if we are aware that there is a time for everything. It is a time now, to understand the writing on the wall. We must see. We must watch. We must sniff. We must smell the air. We must hear. We must decipher the sounds of the voices and words. As thirsty as we are, we must also taste the water, salty or not, knowing that the time will come when the thirst is quenched. As said before, because *there is a time for everything* ... (as the song says).

This sombreness, which resides between the lines and among the words and moods of the poems, cannot exist outside of a context, and that context cannot exist without or outside of what is relative to it. There is something to learn here from these poets. Only the courageous must soldier on now and listen to these poets so that when the time comes, they can teach and teach for real; they can console and console because they know sorrow and what it feels like, as intangible as it is. They can heal because they know the smell of disease and illness. Whatever it is the poets are saying is not of our country only. We are forewarned and therefore we can also forewarn if we allow ourselves to know and to understand.

We will recall from the result of our history that art, of which poetry is part, is a part and parcel of culture. Culture is the dynamism of our consciousness, as we nurture it, live it, make it, and as it expresses our history and our very being through it, we find ways to relate to each other and us to others; it determines our very being – this culture – and now that it does so negatively, it seeks to inspire us to seek and find it in us to be positive. The poets in this anthology have spared no one. If the ideal was reality, we should be saying, if what the poets have said hurts, or inspires anger or makes one to want a fight, one must remember that one's choice is what shapes and makes one, one would therefore have to make wise choices.

The train has pulled out of the platform – it roars on the iron, heating it; it hisses through the landscapes, starry eyed to its dapple forms; it is focused on its destination near to the far distance; it has taken off. What it leaves behind is the silence of our speed, which keeps repeating to us that life is very short. We must never be deluded that time moves; we move. The locomotive of this gone train is the poets of our country. Let's make a way to love and to know them. They are the citizens of this world, which recently shrunk. One of these days, when schools of translation are created, and when the orphan languages emerge and speak, *ho tla shwewa* because we shall hear things we have never ever heard before.

It does feel as if some of the African language poems were thought in English, but written in either of the African languages. If we have declared death to African languages, it is the same as spilling oil on water until there is no more water, but just oil, which of course is no longer oil. It is very difficult to know whether the Minister of Basic Education can hear the deep wisdom of these languages, which, like all other languages of life, are an expression of the unique experiences of the lives lived by those who speak the languages; it is very easy to see from how the African language poets have done here, that there is a deep thirst and hunger to return to the well to drink. We will be wise to know that there is still time and the skill to cleanse the well. The question, Minister, is, if we were to take to the people what belongs to them, is there a political will to do so?

Mona moo ke teng ha se heso,

                              Where I am is not home,

Ke hopotse heso moo ke tsebang,

                              I miss home where I know,

Mona ke heso moo ke sa tsebeng,
> This is a home I know little about,

Heso ketseba ke le ditjabeng tse nthatang,
> I know home when I am with nations that love me,

Heso ke tseba ke le ditjabeng tse ntlhohileng.
> I know home when I am with nations that hate me.[3]

Here, in sorrow the poet reminisces about what could be but what seems to have receded into the distant past. The sorrow comes from a deep sense of loss; but also from a knowledge of what was best. The poet is dextrous with words and Sesotho. What is most welcome here is to experience Sesotho teaching English, that is, when the African languages drown English in African culture. This anthology has created a platform for bounds of possibilities for the shoring up of the diverse expressions of the South African cultural landscape.

There are Afrikaans poems here also. It is necessary to begin to dialogue about language in our country. How must English and Afrikaans become African languages too is the question! In other words, what must we keep doing until all South African languages are an African discourse? When in fact, will it be in reality that all South Africans in their diversity are Africans. When will it be, when we can no longer say: "*Mono moo ke teng ha se heso …*"

Die duitse meneer in
> the German gentleman in

Sy khaki safari-onderbaaitjie
> His khaki safari-undercoat

Gemoonbagde vroutjie aan die sy
> moonbag'd little wife at his side

Trotseer buitengracht braaf
> faces buitengracht braaf[4]

There are light moments between the lines in some poems of this anthology. Read them for relief! At times, the humour catches and dramatises the cruelty of life.

Mongane Wally Serote
September 2015

---

1 Baleka, What do You Know of Tenders and Thieves? Or Cockroaches for that Matter? Poet says the quotes are from www.thaibugs.com
2 Ibid
3 Translations of Sesotho poem: *Ke Hopotse Heso* by Goodenough Mashego
4 Translation by Johann de Lange

Message from the ambassador

The European Union Delegation to South Africa is proud to be associated with the Sol Plaatje European Union Poetry Anthology, now in its 5th edition.

This project is about recording South Africa's oral and written word, about the country's many realities ranging from its deep humanity to its, at times, shocking cruelty, about describing both its unparalleled beauty as well as its many challenges.

In short, it is about providing a platform for South Africa's exciting poets to capture the moment – to hold up the looking glass for us to see South Africa as it is.

In conclusion I pay tribute to all who have contributed to this project – first and foremost the poets, our publishing partner, The Jacana Literary Foundation, and the esteemed panel of judges. Your work is a stepping stone towards a common cultural experience in South Africa.

Roeland van de Geer
EU Ambassador to South Africa

Baleka, What do You Know of Tenders and Thieves? Or Cockroaches for that Matter?

> *"If food is scarce, adolescent cockroaches can live on a very reliable resource – their parents' faeces."*

There are lessons that a parent
can teach a child. The first few steps,
how to listen, read, and write. Seldom
how to be tender as you plunder
and rape, how to deal with the spoils,
the leftovers, something sharp
scraping the bottom.

> *"The New Zealand Y2K Readiness Commission gave out a recipe for cockroaches*
> *in case the world ended on New Year's Eve, 1999.*
> *'Simmer cockroaches in vinegar.*
> *Then boil with butter, farina flour, pepper and salt to make a paste.*
> *Spread on buttered bread.'"*

You are suspicious of concoctions
from the West, for there are countless
ways of nourishing a nation. You
have secret recipes you're unwilling
to share. We're eager to know what lies
squirming in your mind. What's that
bulging under your sleeve?

> *"Scientists claim some female cockroaches prefer weaker partners because they like gentle sex.*
> *A University of Manchester team has concluded stronger male cockroaches are too aggressive and often injure their partners."*

There are consequences, you say,
for not heeding the pliant rod
of your word. In a chamber
echoing an empty order, no king
will want to speak. So you had to
stamp your feet without even grinding
your teeth this time around.
A flick of your hand and the beating
instantly began.

> *"A cockroach could live a long time, perhaps a month, without its head."*

Thugs go through the academy of thuggery. The ABCs
of how to swing a stick, a *panga*. How to aim a gun
that need not be fired, except on a whim. One head
may roll, and another. Yet bodies keep kicking,
running even, as if they weren't missing anything.
Because cockroaches breathe through the holes
in their skin, living on nothing for weeks
on end. But they do, eventually, wilt.

> *"Cockroaches have been present on the earth for more than 400 million years."*

How did you get so far up
that ladder, appearing to know
so little? Perhaps your mind
cannot even go back as far
as Rwanda, when cockroaches
were grafted onto human flesh.

    JIM PASCUAL AGUSTIN

Quoted cockroach facts from www.thaibugs.com/?page_id=137
www.mg.co.za/article/2015-02-14-mbete-eff-are-pawns-of-the-west-who-want-to-control-sa

Veins Cut Open

The veins on maps are thinner
than threads. What courses
through yours runs in mine,

stains all clothing. A piece
of paper that says I belong
might as well be kindling.

A fire like this keeps burning
towards an end the world
has seen too many times.

    JIM PASCUAL AGUSTIN

December in Paris

We've been walking the Paris streets all night
we can buy coffee but not a bed.
Our friend isn't answering,
the last metro ran hours ago.

Sitting behind steamy windows
nursing an espresso, a petite bière,
we watch the cold rise from wet flagstones
the street lights are harsh, yellow.
We leave before they ask us to move on.

Counting the hours to dawn,
smoking each Gauloises Blondes
to the filter, sharing them to make them last,
we're lost in Paris, walking, walking.

It's sunrise, another narrow cobbled street
the houses lean over us, watching,
the sky is a washed out European blue.
I look up and see the dome.

Sacré-Coeur, gleaming in the sun.
I've only ever seen it in
pen and ink drawings on place mats
and on my granny's tea tray.
I know it straight away.

The pavements come alive,
waiters drag out chairs and tables,
we're no longer alone.
We find a phone box and call again,
get directions, jump the metro gates,
ride for free, out to where the migrants live.

                              KARIN ANDERSEN

The Thursday market

In the alleyways of the old town
wild boars lie on pallets
buckets of olives stand in line
piles of cheese perfume the air,
there's pâté de foie gras, truffles, artichokes,
food we can only look at.

The butcher sells sheep's heads for 12 francs,
they're cheaper without the brain.
We boil one with garlic,
eat it with salt and mustard,
share the tongue, the cheeks, the lips,
the eyeballs embedded fat, one each.
Grease on our fingers and faces, we feast.

                              KARIN ANDERSEN

die pad na Klipfontein

as 'n trop bobbejane vroeg in die
middag téén jou langs die teer kom
draf,

dan swenk, koes koes verby jou
hink,

en twee sonkykers ongesteurd bly
bid na bo,

en 'n likkewaan jou pad oorkruis,
jou dwing om stil te hou,

en twee wit perde uit 'n sprokie
spring, hulle sterte lui karwats
voor hulle die veld en bulte vat,

en al die ander diere van die veld
hulle koppe lig waar jy verby hulle
hou –

jou stil betrag – asof hulle reeds
die groot misterie weet,

en 'n arend op 'n hoekpaal sit,
die laatste uitdraaipad bewaak,

jou deurlaat met 'n strak oog,

en jy, net voor die plaashek na die
huis, die rilling van 'n winter in jou
rug gewaar –

dan het dit tyd geword om op te
kyk,

die binneluike oop te stoot.

CAREL AÄRON ANTHONISSEN

Afrika-les

As ek die groen kolle op die mat sit en tel,
vertel Plaaspriester Melité se vrou:

"Daar was 'n tyd, lank voor myne, dat
*Unkunukulu,** die wolke, die lug
en die gevaarlike gruisgat
styf saamgestamp was."

Unkunukulu.

Gestoomde breekmielie vas.
Mens kon aan die sterre raak.
Vanmôre ruik ek die wolke.
Dié wat suurmelk-skifsels maak en
ook dié wat biesmelk-blou
om die klippe vou.

Unkunukulu.

In die aand het die wilde honde
al in die rondte om dié kleibol gekef:

*nke, nke, nke, garu,*** *nke.*

Die lug wat laag hang: die stat se mense
het oopmond kiestevol gevang, gekou,
taai vingers aan wit wolke gesmeer
en sonder dankie sê gevra vir meer.

Nke, nke, nke, garu, nke...

Hulle het dikmelk-wolke losgeskeur
en die lepel laat klingel teen die kookpot.
Sonder dankie sê het hulle gevat.

Nke, nke, nke, garu, nke.

Nou meet die priester se vrou die son met haar oog.
Sy vertel: "een so 'n middag
smyt die vrou wat die kleintjies bad
`n skottelvol waswater
 in die gesig van die lug."

Nke, nke, nke, garu, nke.

Toe krimp die wolke terug.
Vanaand is die lug weer styselstyf.

Nke, nke, nke, garu, nke.

CAROLINE F ARCHER

*Unkunukulu: die eerste Man.
**Garu: hond.

The Phone Call

My grandmother leaves a voicemail.
You're always busy, you never phone.
Crepe paper hands tap-tap
the receiver against her ear, I hear
beat by skin-bruising beat
the metronome of age.
Through the line I listen to
her record the frail betrayal of nerves
the pain in her knees her back
now also in her fingers
all those weary places
without me, the granddaughter
who is always too busy to give her a call.
Until one afternoon when there's
canned pilchard curry cooking
at the neighbours and I remember
after-school buttered toast
sugar in the inkomazi
muskaana biscuits hot-from-the-oven
onions and cloves colouring the oil
and a generous unshakable woman.
I phone my grandmother
to ask for the recipe.

SALEEHA IDREES BAMJEE

Who will?

Child, the day you leave your mother's womb you are cast
    into a land that is shackled;
her flag perpetually at half-mast.
Will you ever live to see the footsteps of childhood behind
    you?
Will you ever know solitude or dream of things beyond
    high walls, barbed wire or barriers?
Will you ever find space for love for a neighbour when all
    that gnaws at you day-in and day-out is hatred?
Will there be olive branches left to offer by the time you
    grow old enough to make your own decisions or will all
    the olive trees be axed, bulldozed and burnt until all
    that remains is
ashes and dust, ashes and dust?
Who will answer for those bones draped in the colours of
    black and crimson?
Who will liberate her; cloak her in white and emerald?

                                        FADWAH BOOLEY

Aleen

Net die vuurgekletter
in my oor
die cabernet se bessie-frank
op my tong
die wolke-wit berge–groen
in my oog
die winter sonstrale helend
op my lyf
die geur van bergsalie gekneus
in my neus

    STEVEN BRESLER

Portrait of a Mother and Indiscretion

My mother smells of indiscretion – in fact she smells of strange things. Not camphor or Zam-Buk; not of anything familiar.

My mother walks slowly, crossing the bedroom in high-heeled shoes. In my grey window I see the sky. In the sky the moon is round. She hides her smile behind the curtain lace and whispers, "My child sees everything."

I'm waiting for her to hang her winter coat. I am eager to glimpse her body. Her buttons fall away. She is kneeling at my bedside, upright. Her hand on mine. It's raining. She is lipsticked and caressing my face. The moon is dead. Her hands don't feel the same anymore. The stars have gone out. I turn and bite her sad hand; she flies backwards. I am loud and yellow laughter. I whisper back, "My mother wears a disguise for my eyes only."

My mother is an old woman. She is no longer young. Yet I smell her indiscretion. I have smelt it on her for days. She has been laughing and smiling without restraint.

SINDISWA BUSUKU-MATHESE

Veldmeens se lied

Toe was dit Januwarie,
en die son was warm en die aarde was kjirkdro,
maar dit was goed, want so had dit gehoort.
dat ees mos'ta sy natuur veldmeens!
En sy eerste twaalf dae had daai waarheid vertel,
die waarheid van die twaalf maande wat voorlê.
Februwarie breing toe 'n koelte,
so asof hy van die see uutgereis had.
Net die veldmeense was toe bekommerd,
want so had dit glad'ie gehoort'ie.
Hy moes gekook'et, dat die aarde behoorlik gebrand had.
Maart, hy't weer so anderster gekom,
winderig, da weer koel, da weer warm.
so asof hy deurmekaar was,
want wat had Februwarie ta nou eintlik gemeen?
Toe kom April vol beloftes,
met onweer uit die Boesma'land,
en bliksemstrale en !xhoeroe en als,
maar helaas nie eens 'n halwe duim,
net stof plat druk en 'n streep oor die Buffels,
dour duskant die Kamiesberge af Kleinzee toe.
Maar Mei, hy had nou geheel die kop gesmokkel,
want alle tekens was daar.
Die pofadder uut die rivier berg-op,
met nuwe sleepsels amper elke dag.
Die rysmiere heeldag doenig,
om die laaste droë stokke te begrawe in moeder aarde,
want so sal dit mosta nodig wees as hy kom!
Maar na die eerste week,
toe weet die veldmeense daar's fout.

Hy had toe nog nie eens amper gekom'ie!
Die kokkewiet had glad in die middagson geroep,
da ooste toe, da weste toe, da noorde toe, da suudwaarts
 sommer ook.
Nie soos hy smôrens op die hoogste klip net weswaarts
 moes roep,
want hy's mosta die mis-voël!
En net toe Mei met al sy tekens van ouds amper om sy tyd
 was,
so in die laaste paar dae van sy bestaan,
toé stoot die brakwater op in die puts,
en die veldmeense bid toe erg,
want dit was die laaste teken nog oor,
een laaste enetjie vir die hoop van lewe,
want toe was als uutgedrô,
Kliphard, Dor, Asvaal!
En alle veld-siele was diep hounger.
Maar op die dag van die winter,
op die vooraand van die geboortedag van Junie, om presies
 te wees,
toe staan die boomstomp-wolk op,
eers uit die suide en toe weer uit die noorde.
En toe kom daar 'n breek,
'n breek van die tyd, want hy was vol.
Vol soos die vrugbare skoot van 'n vrou,
want sy water moés breek.
En die bede wat gehoor was, word geantwoord,
want die geween van die veldmeense had bereik,
die hoogste hemele, tot by hulle sie Skepper.
Hul hoop had gebore in Junie,

en dit was goed, want toe was die slounge al berg-op,
die rysmiere se spense was vol,
die kokkewiet was weer die mis-voël,
en die veldmeense was dounkbaar,
want Junie se vrugwater had mooi gebreek,
Seing veldmeens! Seing!

                ARTHUR BENJAMIN CLOETE

Austin Roberts Voëlpark

Sarbidiornis melanotos,
die kakerneuseend
met sy dalmation-bespikkelde kop
staan statig soos 'n struggle-tannie
wat weet van wag
vér verby die oomblik wat
die punt van alle gewaggery in
die vergetelheid in verdwyn,
sy bonkige buitelyne 'n blerts
teen die backdrop van die Groenkloof-rantjies

die voëlkykers kom en gaan
om te staar na die
swierige bloukransvoël, die
bloedbloeibors van die rooivink, die
doelgerigheid van die bontvisvanger se bek
maar waar hierdie meneer,
die knobbeleend, staan,
staan hy vir niks of niemand
behalwe die sin van staan self –
breedboudig, vasvoetig,
volkome fokken veervoelig.

ECKHARD CLOETE

by die dood van Mikhail Kalashnikof

*"Sowat 250 000 mense word glo jaarliks met 'n
AK47 doodgeskiet.
Kalashnikof het sy lewe lank gedig."*
　　　　　　　　　　　　Beeld, 28 Desember 2013

Eintlik wou hy gedigte skryf,
sê die luitenant-generaal
vier jaar voor sy dood.
Maar die lewe het 'n ander pad
met hom gestap. Dit was nie 'n
paar sensitiewe woordsoekers wat sy
skepping styf teen die bors gedra het nie
maar 'n hele generasie skoorsoekers,
hul drome van mag ingeprent op
die retina, 'n gloeiende kooltjie
op 'n wye filmdoek van vrees en
verkragting in 'n taal selfs magtiger as
die swaard of panga.

'n Uitgewer se guns was oorbodig.
Sy meersterstuk in slegs agt bewegende dele
het spontaan gereis in rugsakke,
vinniger as 'n veldbrand versprei,
van Moeder Rusland na Castro se Kuba en
Noord-Korea langs modderige voetpaadjies,
en uiteindelik opgeneem in die
laerskool-sillabus van Sierra-Leone,
'n klipharde piel van patriotisme,
sekure visier ingestel op die paleis op die heuwel
waar diktators onrustig in hul beddens omdraai,

die septer in die hand van tieners wat
gróótmeneer pronk op die pad
na die wankelrige troon –
'n rooi tapyt van bebloede lyke.

Eintlik wou hy gedigte skryf,
sê luitenant-generaal Kalashnikof.
Maar hoe kan 'n paar digbundels
kompeteer met só 'n nalatenskap? –
'n Hele oeuvre van uitroeiery
wat sy plek regmatig inneem
in die kanon van afkakkery
langs die Bybel en die Koran,
onder die kopkussing van Osama bin Laden,
agter die toe ooglede van
'n duisend-en-een moeders
wat nooit meer slaap nie.

Nee wat, luitenant-generaal,
gedigte skryf is vir die voëls,
vir die kraaie en die aasvoëls
nadat die laaste skote
van die dag weggesterf het.

      ECKHARD CLOETE

natuurlewe, afrika

die duitse meneer in
sy khaki safari-onderbaadjie
gemoonbagde vroutjie aan die sy
trotseer buitengracht braaf

intrepid explorers in donker afrika
terwyl die suidooster mevrou
se pienk laphoedjie van haar
kop wil-wil bevry

gewapen met 'n mastercard
'n ekstra paar sokkies
en 'n skoon gewete
is hul navorsing deeglik gedoen

maar wat hul nie verwag het nie
tussen die opdrifsels van die derdewêreldstad
is die bergie in sy
geïmproviseerde kokon op die sypaadjie:

'n plastiekrob
stadig aan't asemhaal
op die maat van die
wind se nukke

      ECKHARD CLOETE

Die Kaper-naar

Met 'n passievolle gaping
Kom hy nader, gewapen
En sê dis 'n kaping
Één word en ek's ontslape
 "Djou wallet!"
Ek gee dit gelate
 "Djou foun!"
Vat en dink aan die genade!
 "Djou kartape!"
Dank die vader
 "Djou karslietels!"
Ek gee dit verslae
 "Hou ma' djou kar
dis hoe os kaap
hie' innie Kaap in!"

LEONARD ETIENNE CLOETE

A Short Guide to Death

It's late at night. It's dark
in the Old Age Complex.
An ambulance drives in,
stops at the house next door
A quiet voice says something;
another answers.
Doors open; then close.
The wind blows softly.
I can hear the sea.

There is no siren.
This is how I know
there is no urgency,
no hurrying to hospital.
The dead can wait.
There isn't any rush
to take them to the morgue.

When you are old, Death can come like that,
sliding in at the door, quietly,
without a fuss.
However long expected, always
a bit untimely, always in the end
a bit of a surprise.

                    MARGARET CLOUGH

OLD POET

She sits, frail, at a coffee table,
passes me tea and muffins,
shows me sheaves of papers –
poems she has written and
the letters she has received
praising them.

I strain to hear her gentle yammering.
"Poems come to me naturally,
 inspired, fully formed.

"I was a painter too – was offered exhibitions
but turned them down.
I like to keep my work about me.
You can see my pictures hanging on the wall.

"And my pottery, there on the shelf –
all the items beautifully finished.
The studio wouldn't show me how to glaze
I taught myself."

I look back through the window as I leave
to see her pale and withered,
a pressed flower, preserved
in the glass-cabinet of her past.

                        MARGARET CLOUGH

Heritage Site

I don't own this land, but I belong here
and my grandchildren who play on the swings – 17th or
 18th generation.
Are we still called settlers?
Today the mountain dressed in yellow – Bitou,
 bosluisbessie,
this 100-acre wood – they've harvested almost all the trees
but porcupine, mongoose, caracal have all returned,
and shrike, owl, the chaffinches Rhodes introduced.
I know where the animals live, how they move about –
the jackal buzzard twisting the thermals,
when I hear a rush of wings past my shoulder and the
 rufous movement
catches my eye – I know it's the African goshawk.
I stretch my arms to Devil's Peak, to Muizenberg Man;
along the clay track, the boardwalk, reeds and palmiet,
 lowland erica,
a heron lives here, hunts on long legs,
and crows dance a black Matisse circle.
Now through a copse of bluegum –
and along the western boundary where descendants of
 slaves
grow roses and sell compost outside their cottages.
I've seen the water mongoose slink into the grass
and the striped skaapsteker.
April brings showers and the streams of Prinses Kasteel
 begin to flow,
in May mushrooms on the loamy forest floor – pine rings
 and porcini –
where the chaffinches feed.

How Rhodes longed for English birds and deer – you
    could say he pined for oak and elm
but his mines, his railways – Cape to Cairo – demanded
    timber.

Now those trees must all go –

but the chaffinches can stay
and the grey squirrel.

CHRISTINE M COATES

Mapungubwe

The dust rises from the road, the left behind hills
clouds are piling, the smells of potato bush
here in the shade, between the Shashe and Limpopo
an amphitheatre of earth
of rock and rhino.
The ancient animal stands sentry
a threatened species
a baobab
Leopard's Kopje
sandstone, stone walls – perhaps a thousand years
or more.
The opening in the bush promises
vaults and forgotten gold.

The earth here is red, red berries, beads, bangles, ivory
all the while, in the sun, a lone survivor
his face furrowed, holds a sceptre and wants reburial.

An inkling of igneous rock, the Iron Age.
There's the kind of history, of trading wealth
of becoming weak.

This is the place of the jackal –
and those who come after the kill.

CHRISTINE M COATES

Bruidjie van Jemen

Aan wie se hande is die bloed
van die bruidjie van Jemen?
Wie moes die kurf van haar lyf gesien het
hoe sy bang word
moes gesê het:
laat my haar nie aanraak nie?
Wie moes gekeer het
moes gesê het nie my kind nie
nie daardie kind nie
geen kind nie?
Wie het almal kom kyk
hul kenne blink van bruilofsvleis
hoe swartoog Aaeesha
sonder haar ma sonder haar pop
sonder 'n laaste soen op haar hare
haar oë op haar man se skoenpunte
weggelei word?

Wie sal 'n woestyn wegdra?

Die aarde waai haar laaste skoon lug
oor die klein grafte in die sand.

CORNÉ COETZEE

Platipuspaddas

Hul wonings was langs vinnige riviere
in die klein kolke en sloepe en versnellinkies
tussen klippe. Hulle het graag in sagte reën gesit.
Hulle was ligbruin met donker vlekke
geel en geilgeel aan die binnekant van die lede-
mate en glad en witterig by die bors soos riffels
son en skaduwee op 'n rivier.
'n Handpalm groot; snoet stomp, gerond,
vingers aan die voorpote bruin en slank
tone geweb en riviervaardig.
Die mannetjie het sy liefde vir groot, mooi vroue
kwo kwo kwo kwo van lente tot hoogsomer geroep.
Die wyfie het die eiers ingesluk, hoe raar is dit?
Hulle ander naam was buikbroeiers.
Van die paddavissies weet ons byna niks.

Hulle het langs riviere gewoon.
Hulle het graag in sagte reën gesit.

CORNÉ COETZEE

Performance Scale

> *"The startling fact was this: my body was offering a precise physiological equivalent to what had been going on in my mind."*
>
> Joan Didion, *The White Album*

1:

I spent so many years attacking my body,
finding fault in faint abundance, obsessing over every lack
that it didn't surprise me when I woke up one morning
to discover that it was finally fighting me back.

2:

This was the year you kept killing all the machines you owned
and that is what we refer to as a "running motif"
(and *that* is what we refer to as "dramatic irony").

3:

You'll come to,
conked out on some strange cistern in a Southern Suburbs mall,
your legs hinging against the plastic billboard of the bathroom door,
angled in the jamb-like damp cardboard
folded and forced into a full stop.

4:

This is paper as metaphor and limbs as punctuation.
This is the reverse of writing.

5:

You'll find your phone lying, lesioned, next to you,
a fissure fresh down its crustacean container
like a phantom crack. Like a mime at a wall,
bucking but flat.

6:

You're tipped against a nurse
whose prophylactic palm pats nerved and certain on your neck.
You have heard her tell the others that they are good girls.
You are not a good girl
because when she sets you straight on the mat, then the scale,
she only says, "Try not to hurl", then
"You must make a note of your weight".

7:

The zinging technology of your mouth
steams against the frosted door of the consultation room.

8:

She is warm and alive as an urn at the Church fête
and you are the Styrofoam cup
leaning at her tap.

9:

"Look at it this way, at least you'll be skinny!"
is quite a funny thing to say to someone
when you think they could be dying.

10:

You began to let your bob grow unbidden,
split and wrought
because if a part of your physicality still chooses to thrive
who are you cut it short?

10:

You make these kinds of jokes.

11:

You are convinced that the nails and hair of a corpse
inch out past conclusion, intrepid as weeds, eternal as worms,
eyeless and edging in all directions, past even the last right
to scratch into life. This is poetry, I thought,
before I was told that I was wrong.

12:

You retract back into yourself, creating the illusion of growth,
moving like a skirt hitched above the knee, balking as if in shock
pressed against the back of the closest ablution block.

13:

At 27, I became blind in one eye
but didn't realise, because I only notice my mouth.
I thought perhaps a crack had formed between my head
and the cheese-cloth membrane of my disbelief.

14:

Speaking is uncertain and pinpricked.
It is shrouded. It is grief.

15:

Every bad thing that'd happened to me before
was because a man had decided to teach me a lesson
and this is why, after I found out,
I had to reconsider atheism.

14:

You are turning a manuscript into a
fan with the bridging press of pleats.
You are not Keats.

15:

The good doctor made eye contact with me for the whole beat,
which I know is supposed to convey the meaningfulness of the moment
because of my expensive acting degrees.

16:

Raisins injected with water.

17:

Thinned the way paint under the slow drip of turpentine is.

18:

I pick this bed because of its proximity to the TV. I am surrounded by women who are in various states of collapse. One spends each day lamenting the canteen's slopped and unbroiled chicken ala king, sending voicenotes to her daughters to remember to let the cat in. The others cannot walk. I do not want to know them. I do not want to admit that I am one of them. At first, I shuffle, hesitantly, like it's a character choice, until I realise I am not performing and the gimmick has stuck, gammy. My legs lurch and twitch beyond me.

19:

I look up and there is nothing.

I look down at my own arm, which the nurse has stuck so repeatedly, finding me false and veinless, that the blood clotted before it gathered, like I was a boring meeting they wanted to leave and this might be the exit.

I look up and she is staring straight at me.

Her face is wide and aimed. I pull out my earphones but she is whispering. I say her name. She is mouthing something and I do not know the words but I know that what she is saying is help me and I cannot even help myself

which is why I am plugged into a wall like a faulty
Blackberry on charge
which is why I am connected to wet metal that looks like a
clothes horse,
which is why I am making so many Joan Crawford steel
hangers jokes.
This means help me.

I thumb the call button. The station, which
perpindiculates next to us is unlike, myself, without staff.
I use the IV as a cane and I call out but the movement of
my voice is as interrupted as my legs, cramped, boned by
pain. There is a sound here, it rings out, clean and to the
side as a scalpel. Panic is a disinfected metal knife, it slices
me from myself, each thought going into the brain instead
of the mouth, bounced like an email sent to the incorrect
address. The prospect of the seizure is thick and electric
in her bones, I can see it. The day before, her family had
come to visit. Two of them explained how this latest bout
was caused by the evil thoughts she allowed to enter her
head. She must lose them. My own which buzzed, a
constant cortex, old and reliable as a Cortina that has been
veering for years, cutting breaks and ties with whoever
passed me by, stay stuck. I wish I had a demon but I
don't, I have my legs and I run past corn rows of beds to
find some assistance

20:

towards the end.

GENNA GARDINI

Die boekanier van Muckleneuk

Oggendverkeer
somerstortreën
'n trollieman met afvalvrag
dikgeslurp en ekstra swaar
kom deur die kruising aangevaar

Knoophemp om sy heupe gebind
denimbroek wat rafel by die knieë
Sy haarstyl kan ek nie onthou nie
Het hy skoene aangehad?

Sou nie kon sê nie, want sy
bolyf
glansbladperfek
het my blik geheel gekaap.

SUNELLE GEYER

Jo'burg, My Darling

Op die hoogste punt van Mollie Straat kan ek sien
hoe steek die stad haar gesig uit bo die horison
die Telkom toring vorm 'n skerp tollie wat die winter
    wolke donker kielie
die rooi ligte van ponte toring veg die lig
soos die son op kom oor Johannesburg

sy is my darling,
maar nes meeste vroumense
het die stad 'n donker kant:
haar hare is vol bloed
van forced removal
van babas sonder speelgoed
en van letsils agter gelaat
deur Brixton Moord en Roof

sy staan landvas in my hart
sy laat my treur
oor squatters in Yeoville
oor haar miljoene kinders in die reën
oor haar nyaope van smart
en haar hoerhuisies bo Hillbrow se Summit Club
wat oorloop
met die kom van toeriste
wat geweetloos tiet gryp soos sy
met haar bene uitgeput oop lê

op die hoogste punt van Mollie Straat kan ek sien hoe
steek die stad haar tong uit oor die horison
die glaskaste van egoli form 'n refleksie wat die winter
    wolke smelt
die straatsligte van die N1 veg die lig
soos die son op kom oor Johannesburg

SHAWN GREYLING

City Night

At a party someone will get drunk,
climb the curtains, vomit
in the kitchen sink. The shy girl
will try to hold the party together
but in the end she'll snort lines
and then leave with a man –
the one as old as her father.
The weariness of the city
drifting down like fine snow.

In the mirror the man looks
familiar – blurred skin and
blood-veined eyes.
It doesn't matter, he's just looking
for a body and a warm fuck.
Yet he remains tethered
by a thin filament to a dream
he had when he was five:
Superman, flight –
the world unfurling below.

                KERRY HAMMERTON

Die moppie van my DNA

My selstruktuur is 'n avontuur
van Batavia tot die Oranjerivier
Portugese matrose en Hugenote
vaar oor die see op Hollandse bote
vervolg deur Katolieke vaar ek suid
dan weer noord onder Britse pote uit
vate, visse, lekker disse, kundigheid van tuine
/Xam en Khoi ritmes kry ek agter koper duine
in my selle gestoor is baie dinge myne
van Maleise spyse tot Franse wyne
taal, tameletjie, patat en werksetiek,
springbokjag, bokkoms en Hindu musiek,
respek vir moederaarde wat ons voed
suurvy en groenvy en suikerriet so soet
Riesling en Mozart van Duitse protestante
kleur, geur en kennis dans van alle kante.
langsaam leer ek haat hoe werk Britse hoon en baat
kastige beskawing wat suutjies skend en skaad.
gene vergeet nie; tydverloop meet nie
my selstruktuur bly steeds te duur.
geskroeide aarde waai roet oor my voet
steel my goud en my huis en beledig my bloed.
net waar jy stap trap jy op gebeentes
waar mooi plase was en blinke gesteentes
tjoepstil hoor ekke van al my gebrekke
dom en ongeregtig op ons eie plekke
vernedering grief maar kyk die Engelse dief
se welwillendheid behandel jou maar stief
beledig so sedig so gekant teen slawerny
solank hulle ryk word van sweet van jou en my.

chromosome leer te stadig dat die Britte glo
die übermensch is Engels en sy missie kom van Bo
Afrika wil nie toelaat dat ek my lied mag sing nie
my moederland wil nie hÐ wat ander snare bring nie.
weer verloor ek alles, alles wat ek het
weer maer jare na 'n paar kort jare vet
my gene het g'n herkoms om na toe te vlug nie...
waar ek vandaan kom, keer niemand weer terug nie.
my selstruktuur betaal van daar tot hier
alles wat ek is, is 'n mengselkultuur
betaal vir jou verhaal en betaal vir jou taal
verdwyn net oor die horison poedelnakend kaal.
ek hoort nie oppie kontinent nie
mengelmoes is nie gekend nie
weg hier jou rondloophond
voetsek nou of vrek jou stront
weg hier jou rondloophond
voetsek nou of vrek jou stront.

SUENEL HOLLOWAY

A letter from the dead

We must return back to Mapungubwe to trace our ancestral roots. We must return to the pyramids and animal kingdoms to know our origins. We must return to our hunting ways and herding days where farming was the heart of our health and livestock the pride of our wealth. We must return to our own literature to tell the future generation our own stories, music and poetry. We must return to our mountains, rivers and forests of magical powers. We must return to our carnivals and festivals where love was our religion. We must return for the sake of the dead.

MORWAMPHAKA MAISELLA SELLO HUMA

Dipšišamare tša Marikana

Thake o sa gopola koša tša maloba tša mešito gona kua thabeng tša mabadi ne go tuka mollo rekopane re le bodikana re tswere marumo a bogale re tshepile modimo le badimo. ao! atswele mamila le dikeledi dibetsa tša ratata bokatladi gona kua marikana diepapolatinamô bahwela ditokelo eng ke nnete batswetse ba gaotse thari malapa a aparela ke ditlala.diwele dikakapa mašaka a gonama gwa šala digomara le mapodisa ka melato mehlala ya dinyakwa ya sepela le beng ba yona mabetleng. Lefase lona la roroga dimpa ba mošo ba gana go boloka dibe tša bona.

MORWAMPHAKA MAISELLA SELLO HUMA

For my brother

For Zamo

You know how it was like
I left you a dining room floor
and graduated to a bed
after our sister left for varsity.
You know the roughness of our hands
and the fierceness of the sun,
you took the wheelbarrow from me
when you were strong enough
to fetch the crates of cold drinks
for our little family business
all the way next to the taxi rank
and a salon where our mother
played a stokvel.

What I want you to know now
is that there isn't much truth
in the township,
it crumbles like bread on the table
even in schools
children smile for a 40 per cent
and success is a gti
parked next to a tiny house,
brothers measure their success
in whiskey bottles
and brush their big tummies
in a tavern
and sisters fall in love with front seats
and wear off in the streets

like car tyres,
you know how the township is like.

It's a victory to rise above all this,
to survive the streets that gush out blood
and open up into graves,
and even more to move out of the township
to places where mornings come with a sea breeze
where people do not know the smell of poverty.
Poverty has filled our nostrils
we know the stench of unflushable toilets,
just outside the township,
shacks alone tell the tale of a man's suffering.
Do not forget the privilege
of having been close enough
a man can only run away from what he knows
find the truth
do not forget our dining room floor
and don't you dare drive a car
that's worth more than where you sleep.

                    MUSAWENKOSI KHANYILE

Mother

dad built a house in a rural area
he didn't want to die in a township
he thought his soul wouldn't find peace
in such an unsettled place.
you left to stay in this house,
I was in primary school.

now many years have passed
you are worried that you left
even where you should have stayed.
we have a sad relationship
we starve of each other for months
and when you can no longer bear it,
you call for what seems like reassurance,
my heart feels heavy inside my chest
when after months
you call to ask if I still love you.

        MUSAWENKOSI KHANYILE

eenvoud

ek lê onder die oorhang van die grot
drup-drup water uit die klip en bons op
die blare van 'n jong stinhoutboom
en spat 'n sproei-reën op my oop gesig
sneeu lê op die pieke en hange van die Malutis
sien ek teen die kille bloue winterlug
'n helende son
niks kom naby die eenvoud hiervan

geen intellek
geen fancy woorde
geen stadsgeriewe
geen vaartbelynde voertuie
geen argitektoniese vernuf
sal ooit blinker skyn as hierdie
water klip boom lug en son

LARA KIRSTEN

Okungenani

Kunokulibuka liphuma liyozilahl' amathambo
Kunokuvuswa ngiphakelwe ngidle
Ngishaye esentwala ngingazi badleni,
Kunokwembathiswa ngifudumale
Ngingazi bafudunyezwe yini,
Ngincamela usuku lwenkululeko.

Injabulo yokus' ayilingani nosizi lokuhlwa,
Injabulo yokukhany' ayilingani nezinyembezi
zobumnyama,
Ukuhlihlima kwezinqolobane akulingani
Nendlala yonyaka wesomiso,
Isangquma safika saphundla
Kwasal' amahlanga ngavun' amahleza.

Umsinga wamahleza unginsalangile
Amehlo aluvindi ngibon' umebuzo,
Izindlebe zivuza ubomvu angibezw' abangimemezayo,
Izandla zimaqukuvela ngibamb' ufasimba
Imilenze iyavendlezela ingiholela emagunjini okufa
Salusufika nkululeko ngikhululeke.

THANDANANI CHRISTOPHER MABASO

Sola gape

Tlogela go apea potsa
Lefase le eme ka dinao
Tsaroga phoka manaba a kgorong
Nako e go eme ka phefong.

Bokgoba bja monagano bo aparetše bana ba thari
Ba kgolofetšwa lefeela ke marena a nankhono
Ba bona bana ba kgoše wa mpana-palega
Motlhoki yena o tla nkga a sa bola
Ka ge le ya lešidi peni a e tlhoka

Kuši o tla tsoga neng?
Lefaseng la Morena maabane le maloba
Bana ba motho ba timana maloba
Ke molwaodutše lehono
Seragamabje se araba putšišo kua Gaza
Thoka ya makgowa e romela mollo
Barwa ba rwala dibe tša batswadi

        KATISE MAWELA

Kuyoze Kube Nini

Nsuku zonke ngiphila ngaphansi kosizi
Ngiphila ngaphansi kwengcindezi
Inhlupheko kimi ihlezi ibhalwe emehlweni
Nesidingo sami angisasiboni la emhlabeni
Angisasiboni nesidingo sokubekezela
Njengoba sengivele ngaphenduka undabuzekwayo
    emphakathini
Engabe ngempela kuyoze kube nini ngihlupheka
    kulomhlaba
Kuyoze kube nini ngempela abantu belokhu bekhombana
    ngami
Njengoba intokomalo ingasabonwa kweyami impilo
Sekwaze kwaba manzi isifuba
Ngizibuza ngiziphendula ukuthi engabe ngiyophila
    lempilo yosizi kuze kube nini
Impela okwami okwezandla
Ngiyacela nakusomandla 'ze angiphe amandla.

Engabe kuyoze kube nini ngiphila lempilo
Kuyoze kube nini ngihamba ngingena umuzi nomuzi
Ngifuna okuyangasethunjini
Impela lempilo engiyiphilayo ayihlukile neyesihluleki
Ayihlukile neyentandane...

Kuyoze kuphume umphefumulo ngilokhu ngikhala
    ngosizi
Ngilokhu ngikhala ngezinsizi
Ngikhala ngokuphila impilo yokuba yisichaka
Njengoba neningi ligiya ngenhlupheko yami
Abaningi babukisa ngendlala yami
Impela sengiphenduke isibonelo senhlupheko
Sengiphenduke umzekelo wosizi nomunyu
Yize nami lempilo ngingayikhethanga
Kodwa kuyoze kube nini ngilokhu ngikhuma uphuthu
    namanzi
Ngilokhu ngigqoka izingubo ezindala
Ngilokhu ngidla ukudla okudala
Nemithandazo yami ayiphendulwa...

Engabe kuyoze kube nini lempilo yakwamhlaba
    ingihlula...

> MOKOENA MLONDOLOZI

Lenhlupheko Izondlula

Konke lokhu okusihaqile kuzondlula
Lonke lolusizi luzoshabalala
Ngelinye ilanga imizamo yethu iyobonakala
Noma bonke bethi sizophelela kulomjondolo
Noma olwethu usizi bangalushaya indiva kulungile
Phela lenhlupheko yethu seyaphenduka umdlalo wefilimu
Njengoba kwabaningi sesaphenduka abalingisi bendlala
    nosizi
Saphenduka inhlekisa komakhelwane
Saphenduka inkundla yokuhletshwa
Kodwa konke lokho akusoze kwaphuphisa ikusasa lethu
Konke lokho akusho ukuthi siyizihluleki
Ngoba vele empilweni asikahluleki
Mama ngilalele uma ngithi yonke lenhlupheko izondlula!

Yize bonke bathi okwethu okwezandla
Yize ezethu izinyembezi sezaphenduka imvula yemihla
    ngemihla
Noma bonke ebesithembele kubo basifulathela
Bangayigqizi qakala eyethu indlala
Kodwa angeke siphelele kulomjondolo
Angeke siphele amandla
Nayo lenhlupheko izondlula
Akukho okungandluli!!

                    MOKOENA MLONDOLOZI

Ngaphambi Kwezifungo

Sasithembisene izulu nomhlaba
Sasithembisene ukubambisana noma izinto zakwamhlaba zihlaba
Nsuku zonke sasixoxa ngezifiso zethu ngaloluthando
Ngaloluthando sasinamaphupho
Iphupho lethu bekungukuhlala sithokozile
Uthando kithi beluhlezi lubhalwe emehlweni
Sasingayigqizi qakala eyezimfamona
Phela nsuku zonke sasincomana
Sasihlezi sitshelana ukuthi akusoze sajikelana
Ngisho noma abantu bangazama ukusihlukanisa
Ngase ngithembile ukuthi siyohlukaniswa iliba
Ngangizishaya isifuba ngithi ngibusisiwe
Kanti cha! Bengisenga ezimithiyo
Kanti impela angibuzanga elangeni...

Ngaphambi kwezifungo zomshado
Ngangithi uthando lwethu olweqiniso
Ngangithi akusoze lwaphenduka iphupho
Kodwa emva kwezifungo zomshado luvele lwaba umzekeliso
Luvele lwaba umlilo wamaphepha
Lwaphelela emoyeni...

Phela amanga kuloluthando kwase kuyinsakavukela
Ukungathembani kwase kunyukele kwelinye izinga
Ukukhohlisana kwase kuyinto yemihla namalanga
Yingakho namuhla ngiliqalekisa lelolanga
Lelolanga lapho sasimephambi komfundisi
Mhla sifunga izifungo zomshado phambi kwezihambeli zethu
Mhla sisingathwe izihlobo nabangani bethu
Ukube ngangazi ukuthi lowomzuzu uzoba isiqalekiso phambi kobuso bami
Kwakungeke ngizenze lezo zifungo
Kwakungeke ngiqhubeke nalomshado
Njengoba namuhla sesiyinkukhu nempaka
Njengoba sesiphenduke izitha...

Kwakumnandi ngaphambi kokuba senze lendumezulu yomshado
Injabulo yayihlezi ibhalwe ebusweni bethu
Ikhaya lethu laligcwele intokomalo
Bheka manje sesivele saphenduka ikati negundane
Ngenxa yalezifungo zomshado
Kunokuthi sizigcine lezo zifungo
Zivele zawuhlukanisa phakathi wona lomshado
Ubudlelwano bethu buvele bayihlazo
Kwavele kwaphela nokuthi siyizithandani
Kwavele kwacaca manje ukuthi siyazondana
Kwacaca ukuthi akusoze sahlukaniswa yiliba
Kodwa sohlukaniswa yilezifungo zethu
Vele sekuphelile okwethu
Ngiyafisa ukube azange sazenza lezifungo...

Ngaphambi kwezifungo besingamathe nolimi
Sasihlezi sitetemuka ndawonye
Uthando lwethu beluvutha amalangabi
Kodwa manje seluyize leze
Konke lokho kungenxa yalezi zifungo esazenza.

MOKOENA MLONDOLOZI

Dinaledi Tse Ntlenyana

Masea tswelang ka ntle le bohe botle,
Kgasetsang ka ntle bommalona ba tla le sala morao,
Ba tla bona botle boo ka lona,
Kgasetsang ka ntle bontatalona ba tla le sala morao.
Ba tla bona botle boo ka lona.

Kajeno tiisetso ya maphelo e tiisitswe,
Dinaledi tse ntlenyana di tla ka kgotso,
Bohang hleng ke tseo di a nyamale,
Fuparang lerato tse ho tsona, le fuparise,
Dinaledi tse ntlenyana di tla ka tshepo.

Didietsang hle basadi re utlwe,
Medidietsane ha e sisinye difate ntle ho moya,
Alili alili, halala, alili alili!
Medidietsane sebakeng, tsokang matheka,
Didietsang hle basadi re utlwe.

Banna, melodi ha e sisinye dinyonyana dirobeng,
E, bosiu dinonyana di tla tsoha di nyakalle le tsona,
Dirobe di tla sisinyeha hara lefifi lena le letsho,
Nyakallo ya lefatshe ke eo e boneng, baheso,
Dinaledi di tlo bokella lerato pakeng tsa baratuwa.
Lelaletsang mahlo a lona lehodimong,
Thapelo ya lerato e tlo arabelwa,
Dinaledi di tla atomelana ho hohelana,
Dinaledi di tla arohana ho bokella lerato,
Dinaledi tse ntlenyana, dumelang hleng,
Re le amohela ka diatla tse pedi, le batle.

                THABISO MICHAEL MOFOKENG

Ke Hopotse Heso

Mona moo ke teng ha se heso,
Ke hopotse heso moo ke tsebang,
Mona ke heso moo ke sa tsebeng,
Heso ke tseba ke le ditjhabeng tse nthatang,
Heso ke tseba ke le ditjhabeng tse ntlhohileng.

Bana beso ke hopotse heso,
Ha o tseba heno o tla utlwisisa heso,
Ha o sa tsebe heno ithute heno ka heso,
Heso ke habo bashanyana, metlaeng,
O qaboha, o qaboleha, o kakalle ke monate.

Ke hopotse heso, pelo e llela lapeng,
Moo lefafatsane le utullang monate,
Mobu o nkge monate ho utlwahale, ke heso,
Dinko di famohe ho kgaketsa monko monate,
Tsota o tsote beso botsotehi.

Leso lebala le fietswe ka makgethe ho amohela baeti,
Heso ke habo bohle, ke hodisitswe ke bohle.
O mpone ha ke dumedisa, ke dumedisa bohle,
Motswadi e mong le mong ke wa ka,
Kgodiso eso e supa jwalo, heso ke heso.
Ke lakatsa ditshifa, di kae?
Ke lakatsa bobete, bo kae?
Ke lakatsa dikgobe, di kae?
Ke lakatsa dipabi, di kae?
Ke hopotse heso.

Feiye, tholwana e rothisang mathe,
Dikgarika, mafura a futhumatsang,
Mafi, lebese le tiileng ka mafura,
Seqhaqhabola, motoho o monate,
Ke hopotse heso, ke o jwetse.

Difate tsa moduwana tse tswibilang,
Ke tswibitse tswibila ka tsona nokeng eso,
Letsopa le dumelang ho bopa le mpopile,
Ke bopile ka kgaba ka bokgabo wa ho bopa,
Moriti wa moduwana ha ke o lebale.

Tsela e lebang lapeng e a hwehla,
E bitsa motsamai wa yona a e tsebang,
E lekane nna ka mmila o patisaneng,
Wena o ka llela marangrang a siyo heso,
Lehae leso le raha marangrang sa maqhubu a lewatle.

Lehae leso le raha marangrang sa kgomo kgamelong,
Botsa MTN, ha e o beso o tuke,
Botsa Vodacom, ha e o bese o tuke,
Botsa Cell C, ha e o bese o tuke,
Botsa Eskom, o kae motlakase wa bo teng?

Sebariki le Sebaretlane di fula thabeng,
Mantsiboya re ba hama lebese le mafura,
Moya wa thabeng o phutha lebese le qhalehileng,
O a ithola hore o ithotse, heso mane hle,
Kgutso le kgotso di kgotsa kamohelo ya heso.

Letjoi le teng ka hara lengope, moo haeso,
Popoleri e tala eo e thiba difefo tse bohale,
Mabelebele a iponahatsa ka botala,
Bolele bo re ratlantse, re tjheha makgala nokeng,
Makgala a dula eme ka makeke ho kgoroha.

Dikoting tseo ho kgesemetse rona kgolong ya bophelo,
Di ne di kgantshitse dinakangwedi, ho kganya,
Diqhomelankong di phatsima ka botsho ba tsona,
Mafokolodi a phatsima ka botsho ba ona,
Kgwedi e kgantsha dikuruetso tsa diporopotlwana, masea.

Le ha dipoko di ntahla, heso ha ke lahlehe,
Dipoko tsa haeso di ntseba hantle,
Le ha ditsotsi di ntshwara, heso ha ke tshware poho,
Ditsotsi tsa haeso di ntseba hantle,
Ke hopotse dipokong le ditsotsing, heso ke heso.

Meriti ya diotlwana e a theha re hopola habo rona,
Re tlohela kgati, re a phasaphasa,
Re tlohela mantlwane, re a phasaphasa,
Re tlohela diketo, re a phasaphasa,
E mong le e mong o hopola habo.

Masupi a kgabile metseng ya bo rona,
Setulo sa ntate se hloka modudi, o ile boya batho,
Setulo sa mme se hloka modudi, o ile boya batho,
Empa heso ke heso,
Ke hopotse heso, meriti e a theha
Ke hopotse heso, ke o jwetse.

THABISO MICHAEL MOFOKENG

Tsietsi Mashinini

Bitso la hao re le lebetse
Mesebetsi Ya hao ere lahlehetse
Maleme a rona a ho furalletse
Bana ba rona ha ba o tsebe
Re o hopola feela ka June 16

TSIETSI MOKHELE

mad as a broken dish

I'm mad as a broken dish
I'm calm as a sleeping pill
Like a sleeping bitch, I'm gonna break you if you wake me
    up, don't taunt me

Do you know that I feel sick
Do you know that you did this
Like a well fought cause I'm gonna fall away slow bit-by-
    bit, don't push me

My heart is tended to last
My heart is tender like glass
Like shattered glass I'm gonna show my cracks, I won't
    last, don't touch me

It's the hard knocks I can stand
It's the small things that I can't
Like a bloody soldier I'll stand even if it's sand, don't
    push me

                              CHE KGAHLISO MOSHESH

eskom na gezi – eskom and power

when two men from eskom arrived
with the prepaid meter box for installation
two years after the first general elections
they found *mxengu* snoring the afternoon
away in a donga
in the middle of an empty yard
with aloe sprouting into
a dense bush on its margins
after a night of *mqombhoti* and chant
at the chauke's where a girl
graduated from *vukhomba* amidst
drums and clapping to womanhood

when two men from eskom arrived
with the prepaid meter box
to connect *mxengu* to the grid
borrow him some light
he cursed waking up daring them to a fight
and when they asked where the box should go
since there were no walls
he pointed to a pole among those
surrounding the donga
and when they spoke of rains
and the danger of electric boxes in the open
he said to them cursing
borha mhandi, loko u nga swi lavi tshika
chisel a hole on the pole, if you don't want to
leave

                        MOSES MTILENI

We Have Come

We have traversed deserts and forests journeying
Following the echo of distant ululations
They said there is dance and song at Mtileni's
Who said distant streams cannot quench my thirst
We the Ngoveni's have arrived with tins of *snuif*,
The old man's jacket, the old woman's blanket, and a bottle of brandy

Hi mabarhule, makula-nkondo	we of the big foot
Hi masiya-yi-govile yi govela vurhena	we are the valiant ones you leave camping
Hi mafamba-hi-ndzhandzha-wakwe	we are ones who walk on their side of the riverbank

We were blinded by a flower Tintswalo in your fields

N'wina va ka Dzumba wa Mthunzi	you of the shadows and of rest
N'wina va ka Ntila a wu landziwi	you of the path that is not followed

We have come to ask for water
We have come to ask for one who will set the fires in our hearth
We have come, we the valiant ones, we of the big foot, we have come
To you of the shadows and of rest, and of paths that can't be followed
May we have the flower in your fields

MOSES MTILENI

MYEKENI UMNTU UKUBA ANIMAZI

Umntu uyilento ayithethayo.
Umntu'yilento kanye ayicingayo.
Nditsho le ayiphononongayo.
Le ayincekelelayo.
Nale asoloko ethetha ngayo.
Umntu usesi siginci asikhalisayo.

Umntu unzulu ukodlula isiziba.
Uyakuz'ucinge ukuba uyamazi umntu.
Suke emntwini kuphume irhamba/intyatyambo.
Namhlanje ukuwola ngolwandle ekwanga.
Ngomso umntu ukutya ngoowagrazula bamazinyo.

Umntu inene akanakwaziwa lula.
Tyhini bafondini!
Kanti umntu unjani na?
Khawuphinde ubuze lo mbuzo.

Into endiyaziyo ngomntu yile yokuba
Lixoki xa sele exoka umntu.
Umntu uyaxaka.
Sukungxama uthi uyamazi umntu.
Umntu akaqondwa nje nanjani na.
Umntu amaxesha amaninzi ayinguye lo ucinga ukuba
    nguye.
Umntu uyakwazi ukuba ngabantu emnye.
Umntu uyakwazi ukuzibanga engumntu kanti Eneneni lo
    mntu akanguye umntu.

Kanti umntu uyenza njani into enjalo?
Nam mntundini andizazi izinto zoMntu.
Buza kwabanye abantu.

        MADODA NDLAKUSE

Keeping his Shoes

She could not give away his shoes.
The Salvation Army came and took
his carefully ripped jeans
and the suit he wore
to his matric farewell.
And someone else came and took
his out-of-tune guitar and his books.
But she could not give away his shoes
so she wrapped them in tissue paper
(even his worn-out Docs)
and pushed them to the back
of the cupboard.

Some nights she sits
in what was once his room
and remembers his guitar
and suit, once worn.
Some nights she dreams,
not of him,
but of children all barefoot,
running and running,
and although she sees
their need
she cannot give away his shoes.

PAMELA NEWHAM

Lost Girls

(On 14 April 2015 it was one year since Boko Haram's abduction of nearly 300 Nigerian schoolgirls.)

Three hundred-and-sixty-five days have gone by.

Each morning the mother touches her daughter's clothes.
Maybe she lifts the hem of a dress to her lips.
Or she sits and holds an old photograph.
Sometimes she reads her daughter's last school report.
"A hardworking girl who shows great promise."
She will not allow herself to ask the questions in the day
but when it is dark and she is afraid to sleep
because she is afraid to dream, they come to her.
Where are you?
What are you doing now?
What have they done to you?
But, even in the dark,
there is one question she cannot ask.
A rooster crows the first glint of morning.

Three-hundred-and-sixty-six days have gone by.

PAMELA NEWHAM

And Soon

And soon…

Last night I heard a gunshot
And soon we will be hearing the news
We will be wearing our suits
Polishing our shoes
Singing in a church
Closing our eyes
Carrying a coffin
Folding obituaries
Singing in a bus
Standing amongst those lost
Covering our eyes from the sun and the dust
Covering a box with sand
Washing shovels
Washing our hands
Standing in a queue
Eating rice and meat
Dusting our shoes
Watching the game
Drinking our beer

"I heard that my neighbor is sick"…

And soon…

                        MZU NHLABATSI

Mathapelo

The one who prays
Prays
Makes porridge before catching Putco
Gets off at the office park around 6am
She makes coffee for her wages
After brushing toilet seats
She refines her face to smiles

Passionate-looking, she collects tea cups
With tears dripping off lipsticks
She wonders if kisses are real
Like comfort on stilettos
She sings

She sells Tupperware on corridors
Since everyone wants to relate to her realities
They concur
Gossip on the number of kids she has and why she can't afford
They tell stories of how she failed to choose
Ghetto over open thighs

It gets tense when they show up to work
Alone
Make up isn't thick enough to conceal scars
They scream at her for missing crams of their broken hearts
And she reasons
"I can wipe it off," while they face losing their jobs

They dream of babies and prices of designer prams
She thinks of hugs and soul food
They walk tall on scripted emotions
She prays and wonders who Dolce and Gabbana are
between 8 and 5
Mathapelo, the one who prays
prays

        SIZAKELE NKOSI

The mad man

He wears yellow socks
And the sun shines on his feet
He owes no one
Owns nothing but the baggage in his faded white plastic bag
Which he carries everywhere with so much ease
He speaks his mind even to strangers
He speaks to himself
Laughs and sometimes dances to those dialogues
He likes Fanta orange, cigarettes and a Grandpa*
We only talk when he asks for money
And then he would tell me stories about how mothers hide their daughters' innocence in abortion clinics
How George changes into Georgina at night
And the witchcraft activities at house no. 69 where everyone is a "born-again Christian"
These paradoxes happen in his presence
And people are only bothered by his appearance
Hambo' geze wena ungazosidina la**
So he never takes a bath
He says it's madness
Kufana nokuthi ukhiphe umuntu okhulele ehlathini emenze ipresident yomphakathi***
He gets so mad sometimes
escapes to a safe place in the mansions of his mind
where things are as simple as unconditional love
he says he likes talking to me because I give him R2 and sometimes R10
plus I have a nice smile
he always forgets my name and asks me all the time

when I tell him my name is Siza
he laughs whole-heartedly and says
they say you're in love with poetry
I wonder why they haven't declared you crazy, mad woman
All I need right now is my pair of yellow socks to warm my feet

SIZAKELE NKOSI

---

*It's a painkiller in powder form for headache relief.
**Means – "Go take a bath and stop annoying us!"
*** Means – "It's like taking a person who grew up in the bushes and making him president of a community."

I know this

It's that I've lived with it
almost my whole life,
I know this:
the smell of cigarettes
burning brightly and then dim,
slowly.
I still have a clear memory of my grandfather
blowing the smoke out through his nose,
his grey moustache had two yellow streaks.
Yellow as Kaizer Chiefs' home kit
and my father inherited the team
the same way he inherited the vice.

As a kid I used to love the smell of a Stuyvesant,
men watching a game and the table littered with spirits.
This is what it means to be grown up I thought
and I wasn't the only one.
All throughout childhood I had friends who played
into the same scenes when we played house,
like our home lives were the same source material that
  informed
that one script.
The drinking drunk man coming back to an
irritable wife and crying child, dragging on a twig.

I almost outgrew it.
We used to rent a three-room flat
and had a family of four as neighbours.
A man and his wife,
their two kids about the same age as

my younger brothers.
Late Friday you could hear drunk slurs
through the walls and on Saturday morning
I used to watch the man through a curtained window
as he smoked through a hangover,
fascinated by how long and hairy his legs were.
How fucked up his life was.
We used to exchange books and walked to the library
together, a daughter being bounced on his shoulders
another keeping close behind him.
The great comfort of most lives.
We both enjoyed books that had protagonists
that had faults and strong principles.
There were thrillers and romances
filled with what I hoped I'd become:
A dignified simple man
who maybe smoked a pipe, and
wrote celebrated books by a low warm light till morning in
    his study.
How far that dream is now.
In high school the winters
were cold enough to dress my breath
in silk wisps, so clean was the air,
and so clear were my daydreams.
My singularity was undoubtable
though too sensitive to stand huddled with boys
who smoked each other's 2 rands,
in corners the teachers seldom visited.
All throughout the year for three years on weekends
on my evening walks I went past them.

Group after group over the hostel fence
and into a shebeen.
And me never following.
Not the anecdotes, not the inside jokes on Monday.
Solitude was what I chose,
the one comfort of a great life.

How naïve.
I spent the first few weeks of varsity
caught wanting of that muscle
that allows one to seem
confident and excited
about their future even though at present
there is no warmth, no familiar
terrain or sound.

There was no assurance.
And even though I'd understood
that is how life is,
knowing is different, knowing is difficult.
Often nowadays I spend a lot of time
thinking about the men in my life,
the two most important are in the past
their memories made sacred by the
Rest in Peace on their tombstones
and their eerie solemn visits to my dreams.
They were in different stages of their lives
yet they both died young
Suddenly I can see the resemblance between the two.

It's like staring into the mirror,
or looking in while staring out into a scene of strangers
    and friends
smoking and drinking,
knowing that they'd known this the smell of a cigarette
    burning brightly and then dim
slowly.
They lived with it all their lives.
I know it because I've inherited it all:
the vice, the love for theatrics that revolve around a
    sphere,
I never saw it happen just felt it without knowing.
I know this.
Life burning brightly and then dim
slowly,
and unfulfilled dreams disappearing into thin air
like shapeless ghosts.

ZUKISANI NONGOGO

I remember when

I remember when
he stood me in front of the barber
the same way he stood me in front of *incibi*.
Cut it like mine he said
and only then did he turn
to ask me if that's the way
I wanted it.

I have at times
tugged at the leash
straining to be my own man
with my own tradition and religion,
but in front of those two men
I wanted to be my father's son.

ZUKISANI NONGOGO

"Promise from the Elders"

Inside the hut,
Gogo called my name,
her smooth black legs,
resting flat,
on the spread out,
grass mat,

She told me to kneel down,
and lower my head,
forward,

I did as I was told,
her ten fingers,
oily with the smell of sheep fat,
began to gently rub me,
all over the centre,
of my head,

Ndodana,
she called out,
with a laughing smile,
from this day onwards,
your kraal will never be empty,
you'll have plenty of cows,

I agreed,
my head and face shining,
with sheep fat,
in the heat of the day

              LAZOLA PAMBO

Granny. Called 'Ma'

At my gran's funeral, many people ankled
to the knee, crushed in prayer. Others stood,
stared down into her coffin. I could not stand
to go see her. See her go. Sat in the pew, avoided

mom's hisses to pay my respects. Bitchbitchbitch. Reading
the eulogy would be enough. The necklace Ma gave me
before she went was tied on a ribbon round a dead neck
though it was mine. I told everyone I wanted it back

since it wasn't hers anymore. They were afraid of ghosts, like
she had been. We had that in common, she and I. Chose
my black clothes thinking of a quiet grandmother, all black
when I looked down but Ma, she would have scolded

"Too much black! Why you don't wear more colour?
Don't know who taught you how to dress. Go put
something else…" I stood at the pulpit, lowered

the mic

and began

FRANCINE SIMON

Licence

Caramel on the cone. Your mouth
on mine. Sugared lips.

I was redoing my driver's. You told me
no secrets. Sent me to be tested.

You had been driving eleven years. I stood
on an X, waited for the examiner. White

woman with biblical hair. Eyebrows drawn on.
Couldn't see your monster eye. I lost

one point. Then got in the instructor's car.

I smelt this body there. Single
woman crying like a fish.

                              FRANCINE SIMON

Tea

At home, we have no tea tray.
Tea is served in each hand, one by one by hand, cup balanced on saucer
everything all in, already added.
No one asks "Milk and sugar?"
Tea is simply served.
Though it must be brought to the guest properly
accompanied by Marie biscuits or Eat-sum-mors.

Tea is my job. I know it well.
my godfather – tea black, two sugars
my aunt – tea (hot milk!) and quarter sugar
my father – tea double sugared, two sugars boiled
he takes his tea with the bag in milk, then more boiled
water added after. He told me his grandfather warmed the
cups with hot water before making tea, which apparently
is the proper way.

He never said which grandfather, which side.
Was it his father?   I don't know
I don't know   why I wonder about that.

I take tea but never drink it.
You can always find a cold cup and know it's me.

FRANCINE SIMON

Lament for the Stones

No longer sure-footed
after my father's death,
some days I was brought
to tears
for the smooth round rocks
lying motionless
in the riverbed.

Over millennia they kept still,
had their edges knocked off,
until scoured sleek,
they lie ovoid, oblong, squat
and suffer in stoic silence
the floods and droughts.

Perhaps they delight in the lizards,
the leguan,
the dragonflies,
the dainty steps
of the Klipspringer.

                 ANNETTE SNYCKERS

Stopover

Like carton cut-outs, row upon row,
the mountains shift past the car window –
bruise-blue, grey-blue,
to the palest shade of sky –
we travel through a land bereft of rain
where poplars on farms
flutter gold and amber
and palm trees lean in the wind –
tall and tolerant, they wave
black shadows over solitary white houses.
The dirt road slithers like a snake through dips
and over ridges of the foothills –
far ahead a car drags a streamer of dust
through the afternoon heat.

Four hours from the city
my mind leaves behind the clutter,
content to hum in thinking
of nothing much –
and how tonight I'll sleep in a place
where stars splutter silver light
over a black velvet night
and where the church bell strikes –
every quarter hour
that remains of my life.

ANNETTE SNYCKERS

The Button Tin

My mother saved
her buttons in a tin –
they kept me busy when
I was a thin small girl –
sorting, selecting,
red ones,
round ones,
pearly ones,
plain ones.

I saved that tin –
so many buttons
that never
got sewn back on again,
bought for a dress
that was never made,
or cut off
a beloved garment
that was worn-out.

My life
is a tin of buttons –
I sit with it on my lap now,
sorting, selecting,
trying to find among
dull ones,
worn ones,
broken ones,

the shiny ones.

ANNETTE SNYCKERS

Rorschach Liggaam

Met passiewe pyn
skiet die mitologiese ink
my vol van my storie.

Die blatante spore
van vleeslike oorlewing
in konstante gedaantes geëts.

        DAVID C STEYN

postpartum

in haar turkoois kamerjas
        toets sy die water in die roomgeel bababad
met 'n skurwe elmboog
        die poeier staan gereed die lammerwit doeke
so ook die skottelgoed in die wasbak ingeseep
        teebekers taankleurig uitgevoer
beskuitkrummels 'n pappery op die bodems
        geen water kom uit die krane nie
net 'n hol
        geborrel van niks
bra's broekies en jockeys
        bont vullis
die strykplank kners
        onder ongestrykte wasgoed
die hond modderspoor
        al weer op die mat
die kat doop
        sy gebied met vrank pis
'n begeerte skiet sy onkruidsaad in haar
        die baba brabbel in sy biesiemandjie
sy skiet
        die badwater uit

                        GISELA ULLYATT

vir 'n uiltuin

*" I must Create a World, or be enslav'd by another Man's.
I will not Reason & Compare: my business is to Create."*
William Blake

road to mecca
nadat die son agter karoobossies nagkabaai
sing sy vir haar sement-uile
versamel groen bottels vir hulle oë
sing sy vir haar boeddhas
kamele en wyse manne
die pad na die heilige stad loop dood
in hierdie godlose stofstrate
in die kele van dorpenaars
in porseleinkoppies rinkel skinderstories

this is my world
in haar tuin geen rose nie
net 'n huis met 'n geel voordeur
wat na grofgekleisterde vertrekke oopskarnier
haar vader ritsel soos 'n tolbos
waai teen haar binnekamer
soms flits hy steeds in donderstorms
sodat sy lanferlappe oor haar spieëls moet hang

beneath a burning sun
oranje son rooi plafon
vergruisde glas in consol-flesse
eerder sou sy laventel
teen verganklikheid wou plant
maar sy drink nagmerries uit koue kruike

would not we shatter it to bits
lug water vuur en grond
onder draai voorouergeeste rond
sy roep moeders uit die droomtyd
vaders uit die dae van die nonnetjiesuil
hulle eggo haar verguisde naam
oor die kompasberg
tot in die vallei van verlatenheid

through this same garden after me
wanneer die lyksak van slaap haar lyf toerits
droom sy van peperboomtakke
in olieverf gedoop
droom talismans gegiet uit nuwe glas

so when at last the angel of the darker drink
hoe roer die engel die water nou
voor sy deur daardie heiligheid waad
haar oogholtes sing
sonder groen glas

                    GISELA ULLYATT

Streetclass Diseases

Abeeda's toothless mouth sprays saliva as
she paints a picture of her thirteen years
on Cape Town's streets. He feels her spit in
his face, on his nose, on his lip, arousing
his middleclass concern over streetclass
diseases. At sixty two, she's never been
to a doctor or hospital; he goes twenty times
a year. Distracted by her dark purple
gums, he misses part of her sermon chastising
him for his pagan life of walking past sick
children drowning in ponds and admiring
his large shadow on cave walls and buying
signed first editions of dead poets while
old women starve on Cape Town's streets. She
tells of her walk with her god, her simple
life beneath bridges, clearly boasting
about her immunity to his diseases. He offers
her cash. She scoffs and carries on digging
through the garbage bin where he found her.

                              ATHOL WILLIAMS

illegal

you ask only for a square of oxygen
a patch of sand and strong legs to run
your Gucci bags strung like silver charms
on a bracelet
as you melt into shadows darker than your skin
and wait for the coast to clear
to return, unpack
and set out bags
set out bags
and when the crowds go home
a place to lie down
to dream the nightmare of la mer
and the lucky break that got you here

SUE WOODWARD

Straatkindnar, 'n skildery

Onder narrekap: veelvuldige profiel om te profiteer,
   na-lopers op elke yskoue hoek, hart en voete seer:
   hare rooi vulgêr; geelkant, sonkant, groenkant, skadukant
   dooie oë geportretteer: vreemd wit en glasig; die hand
klein en koud en bewend, 'n dier vir weerlig bang.
Begeerverhale duisende; pyn-verdoesel geskilder en gevang:
skimme-geskuifel glo: nar wees is profiteur.
Die skilder egter koester dwarrel-blaar-vergetenheid vir 'n
   ewigheid:
Appels-lemoene- rooiwyn-druiwekorrel-stillewe ten spyt!
Wie oorlewe in strate, maar snoesig tot skildery geverf,
het tyd oorwin, 'n ewigheid geërf!

                                      FRANK WRIGHT

Biographies

Jim Pascual Agustin writes and translates in Filipino and English. He grew up in the Philippines and moved to Cape Town, South Africa in 1994. His work has appeared in, among others, *Rhino Poetry*, *Burnt Bridge, GUD Magazine*, and *Modern Poetry in Translation*. His first short story collection in Filipino, *Sanga sa Basang Lupa*, and his seventh poetry collection, *A Thousand Eyes*, will be released in Manila in 2015.
His ramblings can be found at www.matangmanok.wordpress.com.

Karin Andersen was born and raised in Zimbabwe, and then lived in France, Tunisia and England as a young adult. She settled in Cape Town half her life ago, and thanks to her most recent part-time job she has learned that she probably should have spent her life selling second-hand books instead of looking after children, plants, backpackers, translation projects and websites.

Carel Aäron Anthonissen is a theologian and current director of the Centre for Christian Spirituality, founded by Archbishop Tutu in 1986. Writing poetry from his youth, it began a permanent vocation during a study period in Germany in 1990. The poet has already published several poems in English in a series of anthologies on Africa, war and love by the novelist and poet Patricia Schonstein. With the help and support of Marlene van Niekerk (writer/poet) he is currently preparing a first own collection of Afrikaans poems.

Caroline F Archer grew up on a farm in the Orange Free State in the late sixties. She loved the outdoors and riding on horseback. Caroline was the Dux Scholar at a small-town Free State School, Sarel Cilliers, Koppies. She studied languages at the University of the Free State and passed the course with distinction. Her coursework included Afrikaans, English, German, French, Philosophy, Psychology as well as Sociology. Her research of Dutch poets was awarded with the Tafelberg Award for Excellence in Afrikaans and Dutch and she was elected as member of the English, Afrikaans and Dutch study groups. She devotes her leisure time to the care of mentally and physically challenged children.

Saaleha Idrees Bamjee is a freelance writer and photographer who lives and works in Johannesburg, South Africa. She has an MA in Creative Writing from Rhodes University, Grahamstown. Her short story, 'Out of the Blue', won the 2014 Writivism Short Story Prize. More of her work can be seen at www.saaleha.com.

Fadwah Booley from Cape Town, is a borderline recluse, who discovered her love for poetry at 14 after reading an article about a boy brutally killed in the Middle East conflict, which inspired her first poem and incessant journal writing. Before heading off to study Science at Stellenbosch University she ceremoniously burned this journal and abandoned writing. Her love affair with yoga has been a catalyst for rediscovery of her true self, which has allowed her to tune into her innate love for writing. When she's not cultivating her introverted self or tending to cells in the laboratory to pay the mortgage, she just sits and mind melds.

Steven Bresler. This 63-year-old writer is a practising lawyer in Citrusdal, Western Cape. He has a passion for poetry and has written more than a thousand poems, some of which have been published over the years. He and his wife, Carla love to travel and he also writes travel journals. He enjoys playing the guitar and writing new songs. He has received three national awards for gospel music. The sounds of strings and words transpose him into new worlds and other dimensions.

Sindiswa Busuku-Mathese is a young poet born in 1990, based in Durban. She has recently completed her Master's at the University of KwaZulu-Natal.

Arthur Benjamin Cloete lives in the rural town of Concordia in Namaqualand. After school he studied Marketing in Cape Town and later started working at a multi-national insurance company. In 2012 he returned to his native Namaqualand to pursue his passion for photography and farming. After doing freelance writing for local newspapers, he worked in the field of conservation on various community-based projects. He is currently focusing on his farming and photography full time, and has started writing as well, which is inspired by the rich cultural heritage of his people and the natural beauty of Namaqualand.

Eckhard Cloete is a thirty-something who lives in Cape Town. A couple of years ago he sold his soul to the advertising industry, but all he really wants to do is to perfect his single backhand on the tennis court. Some of his poems have been published in the *Groot Verseboek*, *Nuwe Stemme 3*, *New Contrast* and *Bunker Hill*. Eckhard is a self-admitted stationery fetishist with a particular weakness for fountain pens.

Leonard Etienne Cloete is 27 years old and studies at Stellenbosch University. His passions in life are nature and writing. He writes poems whenever the inspiration strikes him. His greatest influence is probably D. J. Opperman.

Margaret Clough is a retired soil chemist and science teacher. She has had poems and short stories published in various journals. She is the author of two collections of poems: *At Least the Duck Survived* and *The Last to Leave*, both published by Modjaji Books.

Christine M Coates has a Master's degree in Creative Writing from the University of Cape Town, is a writer and poet with an interest in life-writing and memoir. Her poems have been published in: *New Coin*, *New Contrast*, *Carapace*, *A Hudson Review*, *scrutiny2*, *Deep Water*, and *Cambridge Conference of Contemporary Poetry Review* and *Africa Focus*. *Homegrown*, her debut collection of poems, was published by Modjaji Books in 2014. Her story, 'The Cat's Wife', was highly commended in the anthology *Adults Only*, and she has a novel under review. She is a member of The Grail Women's Retreat Group and Finuala Dowling's monthly poetry group.

Corné Coetzee has worked in journalism for 30 years; either permanently or as a freelance writer and sub-editor for several publications including newspapers such as *Die Vaderland*, *The Citizen*, *Beeld* and *Rapport*, and consumer magazines such as *Baba en Kleuter*, *Rooi Rose* and *Vrouekeur*. At present she specialises in green articles aimed at consumers. She recently completed a Master's degree in Creative Writing at the University of Pretoria. She is married and lives with her husband and one of her two daughters in Johannesburg.

Genna Gardini is a poet based in Cape Town. She won the DALRO *New Coin* Poetry Prize and was one of the *Mail & Guardian*'s 2013 Top 200 Young South Africans. She is the co-founder of independent theatre company Horses' Heads Productions and currently works as a lecturer at City Varsity's Acting Department. Her first collection of poems, *Matric Rage*, will be published by uHlanga in late 2015.

Sunelle Geyer (Swanepoel) was born in Kimberley in 1974, grew up in Boksburg and matriculated from the Afrikaanse Hoër Meisieskool, Pretoria. She studied at the University of Pretoria and teaches intellectual property law at Unisa. Her favourite timeout activities include reading, swimming and spending time with her husband and their two daughters.

Shawn Greyling. For the past six years Shawn Greyling has worked as a self-taught freelance wordsmith specialising in journalism but also writing short fiction and scripts for television – the latter started as a love affair in 2012 when Shawn was contracted by a Nigerian production house to screenwrite the country's version of the hit reality TV game show *Survivor*. The author primarily writes in English but finds it easier to write poetry in his mother tongue, Afrikaans. His work has been published in *Playboy* (short fiction and hard journalism), *GQ* and South African Airways' award-winning in-flight magazine *Sawubona*.

Kerry Hammerton lives in Cape Town. She has published poetry in South African and British literary journals and anthologies. Her debut poetry collection, *These are the lies I told you* was published in 2010 with her second collection, *The Weather Report* in 2014. More on her work is available on her website, www.kerryhammerton.com.

Suenel Bruwer-Holloway has raised many children and taught many more. Her plays for youth have been published by Junkets and her poems by Quickfox and African Sun Press. She lives in the country and works as an editor and ethnographic researcher, teaches, cooks vast meals, gardens and walks dogs every day.

Morwamphaka Maisela Sello Huma grew up on the dusty streets of Moletlane in Zebediela. A poet and writer, who started writing and performing at the age of 12, Huma is truly inspired by the '80s movement of protest poetry.

Musawenkosi Khanyile is a Clinical Psychology Master's student at the University of Zululand, who developed a passion for poetry in high school. Born in a small township called Enseleni, Khanyile currently resides in Pietermaritzburg. Some of his poems have been published in literary magazines and journals including *New Coin* and *Prufrock*.

Lara Kirsten is a pianist and performance poet. She holds a Bachelor's degree in Music (honours) from the University of Pretoria. As a solo pianist and accompanist for singers and instrumentalists she performs all over South Africa. As a poet, she has performed in the Netherlands and at various venues in South Africa. Lara has performed at the

Wakkerstroom Music Festival, the McGregor Poetry Festival, the AfrikaBurn Festival in the Tankwa Karoo, and the Woordfees in Stellenbosch. She belongs to the Eastern Cape poetry group, Ecca, and has recorded a CD of her own poetry.

Thandanani Christopher Mabaso is a humble man who is a tool-making apprentice student at Durban Coastal College under NIMS standard. He is a hard worker, who doesn't talk a lot but enjoys most of his free time reading books and newspapers. He also likes to write poems, short stories, novels and drama in IsiZulu. He likes meeting new people to discuss problems facing them. He enjoys playing soccer as well.

Katise Mawela is a professional nurse who is fascinated by the spoken and written word. He has been writing poetry from as long as he can remember. Most of his poetry has appeared in *Tribute* magazine. He now writes only under inspiration and chooses to meditate most of the time.

Thabiso Michael Mofokeng was born in Qwaqwa, Free State. He has facilitated various workshops in poetry and prose and is the editor-in-chief of Metjodi Writers. He is the founding managing director of Mosa Media and Book Distributors (Pty) Ltd and the founder of Thabiso Mofokeng Writing Foundation. He is the treasurer of Free State Writers Forum. A professional writer and editor, he has edited for many publishing houses. His work has been included in various anthologies and journals, while some are prescribed by the Department of Education for South African schools. He is currently doing a Master's degree in Creative Writing at Rhodes University.

Tsietsi Mokhele is a poet, writer, and events and community development programme manager. He is a land rights, gender, cultural and language activist who is passionate about preserving local languages for future generations. He is also a founding member of House of Siza – a non-governmental organisation that seeks to change people's lives through words. Some of his poems have been published by *ITCH Online* magazine (Issue 3 and 4), *Poetry Project*, *Poetry Potion* and *Love letters to My Child*. He is currently working on his debut collection of poems in Sesotho.

Mlondolozi Mokoena. Born on 22 September 1994, he is a young writer, poet and an author of a Zulu poetry anthology titled, *Izinkondlo Ezimidwayidwa*. After completing Matric in 2012, he went to Boston City Campus and Business College where he studied for the Certificate of Media Consultant in 2013 and in 2014 he studied for a National Certificate in Paralegal Practice. Presently, he is a Debt Recovery student.

Ché Kgahliso Moshesh is a freelance writer from Cape Town. His short story, 'Wat Agter Ons Is Onder Ons', won the Wits MSc Literature Award in 2013. He is currently studying Medicine at Wits University.

Moses Mtileni was born at Nkuri-Tomu village in Giyani, Limpopo. His poems have appeared in *Botsotso*, *Poetry Potion*, *Timbila* and the *2014 Sol Plaatje European Union Poetry Anthology Vol VI*. In 2010, he self-published two anthologies of poetry, *U ya va rungula* (Xitsonga) and *When the Moon Goes to Rest* (English).

Madoda Ndlakuse was born in Mdantsane and grew up in Port Elizabeth. He is well known for his social commentry poetry and is regarded as one of the best IsiXhosa perfomance poets in the country. He is often invited to perform and be the Master of Ceremonies at weddings across the country. Madoda is a writer, poet, interpreter, reading initiative activist, the founder of Eastern Cape Book Festival and Cream of Literature (Ingqaka Yoncwadi) – both are initiatives that seek to revitalise culture and the future of reading. His latest poem, 'Imihlinzo', is currently enjoying airplay @SABC Umhlobo WeneneFm B.E.E. show. His dream is to help primary school children have an experience of poetry, theatre and storytelling so as to spark their love for reading.

Pamela Newham has worked as an English teacher, journalist and features editor. She has published three novels for young adults. *Three Blind Dates* was runner-up in the Maskew Miller Longman Literature Awards for 2010 and her latest book, *The Klipspringers* (OUPSA) is on the Department of Basic Education's catalogue for Grade 7. Her poems have been published in several anthologies and journals. 'Third Beach, Port St Johns' was shortlisted for the Sol Plaatje European Union Poetry Award for 2012. She lives in Hout Bay and gives lectures and workshops in journalism and writing for children.

Mzu Nhlabatsi is a photographer, poet and visual artist, born and raised Johannesburg. He has been writing poetry since his teenage years. Nhlabatsi grew up in Soweto, raised by his father Mzwakhe Nhlabatsi, a fine artist and graphic designer. His writing is not only a means of expression but a mechanism for dealing with his inner turmoil and life situations. After many years of writing, Nhlabatsi is now looking to share his work with the world in an effort to connect with those dealing with the same internal and external issues.

Sizakele Nkosi is a published poet, lyricist, guitarist and a mother from Soweto. She works as an IT networking specialist. She is the founding member of House of Siza, an NPO that changes people's lives through literature. She took part in the 2012 and 2014 Polokwane Literary Festival and 2014 Northern Cape Literary Festival as well as the Vhember International Poetry Festival in 2015. Her work has been published in the journal, *Timbila*, and the *Sol Plaatje European Union Poetry Anthology* for 2014. She is presently working on her debut poetry music album and a collection of poems.

Zukisani Nongogo was born in the Eastern Cape in Mount Ayliff. He is an aspiring writer currently completing his final year as a Theatre and Performance student at the University of Cape Town.

Lazola Pambo lives in South Africa and is a lover of the written word. His works have been published in *The Kalahari Review*, *Aji Magazine*, and the *2014 Sol Plaatje European Union Anthology*, among several literary magazines. You can catch him on Facebook and Twitter @ LPambo.

Francine Simon was born in 1990. She was the firstborn to Indian Catholic parents and grew up in Central Durban. She began writing poetry at the age of 15. She completed her Master of Arts (summa cum laude) in Creative Writing at the University of KwaZulu-Natal in 2013. She is a doctoral student at Stellenbosch University. Currently, her poetic influences include Chelsey Minnis, Ariana Reines and Harryette Mullen. Her writing has been described as bizarre and lyrical. Her unpublished collection is called Shadow Sounds.

Annette Snyckers is a poet and visual artist living in Cape Town. She studied literature (English, French and German) at the University of Pretoria and later Fine Art at the University of South Africa. She was a high school teacher and translator before dedicating herself to the visual arts. She is a painter and graphic artist working in oils and mixed media.

Annette writes in both English and Afrikaans. Her poems have been published in literary magazines and online in *Aerodrome* and *The Stellenbosch Literary Project*. Her work has been selected for the following anthologies: *Difficult to Explain* edited by Finuala Dowling, *For Rhino in a Shrinking World* edited by Harry Owen, *The Sol Plaatje European Union Anthology* 2012, 2013 and 2014, *McGregor Poetry Festival Anthology 2014* edited by Patricia Schonstein.

David C Steyn, or Karel Kopbeen, is a poet, writer and musician. He was born and lives in Pretoria. He is currently studying Language and Literature (Creative Writing) at Unisa. He has written several entertainment articles and reviews for publications such as *ATKV Taalgenoot*, Mahala.co.za, *Perdeby* student newspaper and SAMusic. His short stories and poetry has been featured in *New Contrast – the South African Literary Journal*, *Ons Klyntji*, *Expound*, *Jip*, Alt.SA online magazine, *Prufrock* and on LitNet. His independent debut poetry collection, *Bloeddig*,

was published in 2012. He was also a founding organiser and co-owner of Die Dowe Digters, a monthly poetry and music session event hosted in Pretoria.
Links: @KarelKopbeen on Twitter
www.reverbnation.com/karelkopbeen on Reverbnation
www.facebook.com/KarelKopbeen on Facebook
www.litnet.co.za/Author/5454/Karel%20Kopbeen on LitNet

Gisela Ullyatt was born in Bloemfontein. She studied languages, and received her PhD in English in 2013 at NWU. She currently writes literary blogs for versindaba.co.za, and does interviews with poets for the same website. She also teaches English at the University of the Free State, and writes book reviews for *Woord en Daad*. Others have appeared in *Volksblad*, *Die Burger* and *Beeld*. She was an organiser of some of the poetry events for The Free State Poetry Festival's Boekefees in 2015. Her poems have appeared in local and international journals, and in *Nuwe Stemme 5*.

Athol Williams is a poet and social philosopher from Cape Town. He has published two volumes of poetry and a children's book, *Oaky and the Sun*. His poems have been published in anthologies and literary journals in the UK, USA and South Africa. His most recent readings were at the SANAA Africa Poetry Festival, AfrWEka Poetry Festival and at the Sackler Museum, Harvard University as a participant poet in the international "here, without" project that dealt with the Israel-Palestine situation. He holds five degrees from Harvard, MIT, LSE, LBS and Wits, and is currently registered at Oxford.

Sue Woodward is a writer and editor of educational material and children's fiction. She is passionate about poetry as a creative discipline and has been writing and reading poetry for many years. She has been published in *Sesame*, *Carapace*, *New Contrast* and *Aerodrome*, first as Susan Mahoney and latterly as Sue Woodward. Sue lives in Muizenberg, a short walk from the sea, the mountains and the *vlei*. She walks on the Zandvlei estuary every day with her dogs and this space is the inspiration for much of her poetry.

Frank Wright was born in Johannesburg on 9 October 1936 and attended Vorentoe Hoërskool where he was appointed head boy of the school. He studied at the University of Pretoria and attained a Master's degree in Afrikaans-Nederlands with a thesis on Marthinus Nijhoff, tiltled, 'Die Bybelse verwysing as struktuurelement in die poësie van M. Nijhoff'. He taught at various schools and also lectured Afrikaans literature at Normaalkollege van Pretoria, a teachers' training college.

He has two self-published poetry books: *Ink druppels gebloei* (Xlibris 2012) and *God Loves Coition* (Jotha 2014).

What is the European Union (EU)?

The EU is a unique economic and political partnership between 28 European countries* that has delivered half a century of peace, stability and prosperity; helped raise living standards; launched a single European currency; and is progressively building a single Europe-wide market in which people, goods, services and capital move among Member States as freely as within a country.

Created in the aftermath of the Second World War, the first steps taken towards a union were to foster economic cooperation. Since then, the union has developed into a huge single market with the euro as its common currency. What began as a purely economic union has evolved into an organisation spanning all areas, from development aid to environmental policy.

The EU actively promotes human rights and democracy and has the most ambitious emission reduction targets for fighting climate change in the world. Thanks to the abolition of border controls between EU countries, it is now possible for people to travel freely within most of the EU.

How does it work?

EU Member States have set up institutions to run the EU and adopt its legislation. The main ones are:

---

* Belgium, Bulgaria, Croatia, Czech Republic, Denmark, Germany, Estonia, Ireland, Greece, Spain, France, Italy, Cyprus, Latvia, Lithuania, Luxembourg, Hungary, Malta, the Netherlands, Austria, Poland, Portugal, Romania, Slovenia, Slovakia, Finland, Sweden, and the United Kingdom.

- The European Parliament (representing the people of Europe)
- The Council of the European Union (representing national governments)
- The European Commission (representing the common EU interest)

Size & Population

The EU is less than half the size of the United States covering some 4 million km². In terms of size, France is the EU's largest country and Malta its smallest. The EU has a population of close to 503 million people – the world's third largest after China and India.

The EU's economy

Operating as a single market, the EU is a major world trading power. EU economic policy seeks to sustain growth by investing in transport, energy and research while minimising the impact of further economic development on the environment. Measured in terms of the goods and services it produces, its economy is bigger than that of the US.

EU symbols
- The European flag – The 12 stars in a circle symbolise the ideals of unity, solidarity and harmony among the peoples of Europe.
- The European anthem – The melody used to symbolise the EU comes from Ludwig Van Beethoven's 9th Symphony composed in 1823.
- Europe Day – The ideas behind the EU were first put forward on 9 May 1950 by French Foreign Minister

Robert Schuman. This is why 9 May is celebrated as a key date for the EU.
- The EU motto – "United in diversity".

The EU & South Africa – a partnership of equals

Since 1994 the growing relationship between South Africa and the EU has been underpinned by the Trade, Development and Cooperation Agreement (TDCA). Closer ties between the two parties were consolidated in 2007 with the establishment of the EU-SA Strategic Partnership.

This partnership, the only one of its kind with an African country, is centred on enhanced political dialogue around issues of shared interest including climate change, the global economy, governance, bilateral trade, and peace and security matters. In line with this, its action plan encompasses sectoral cooperation on a range of issues such as climate change, environment, education, science and technology, space, trade and migration.

Annual summits, as well as ministerial and senior officials' meetings steer the partnership, along with the EU-South Africa Joint Cooperation Council. They provide the occasions to discuss current bilateral, regional and global issues.

Trade & investment

The EU remains South Africa's largest trading partner and in 2013 accounted for 25.57% of the value of South Africa's merchandise trade (imports and exports). In turn, the EU, in value terms, remained the biggest source for South Africa's imports, accounting for 29.29% of South Africa's total imports in 2013. EU countries are also the source of some 80% of foreign direct investment (FDI) stock in South Africa.

Development cooperation

The EU remains an important development partner to South Africa, providing significant external assistance funds. The EU's total indicative grant budget for South Africa for the period 2014–20 amounts to some €250 million. It is complemented by a €416 million loan finance envelope from the European Investment Bank (EIB) as well as grant funding from the EU Member States.